CAMPAIGN • 242

METZ 1944

Patton's fortified nemesis

STEVEN J ZALOGA

ILLUSTRATED BY STEVE NOON

Series editor Marcus Cowper

OSPREY PUBLISHING
Bloomsbury Publishing Plc

PO Box 883, Oxford, OX1 9PL, UK
1385 Broadway, 5th Floor, New York, NY 10018, USA
Email: info@ospreypublishing.com

OSPREY is a trademark of Osprey Publishing, a division of
Bloomsbury Publishing Plc

First published in Great Britain in 2012 by Osprey Publishing

Transferred to digital print-on-demand in 2019

Printed and bound in Great Britain

ISBN: 978 1 84908 591 5
PDF e-book ISBN: 978 1 84908 592 2
EPUB e-book ISBN: 978 1 78096 043 2

Editorial by Ilios Publishing Ltd, Oxford, UK (www.iliospublishing.com)
Page layout by: The Black Spot
Index by Sandra Shotter
Typeset in Sabon and Myriad Pro
Maps by Bounford.com
3D bird's-eye view by The Black Spot
Battlescene illustrations by Steve Noon
Originated by Blenheim Colour ltd

The Woodland Trust
Osprey Publishing supports the Woodland Trust, the UK's leading
woodland conservation charity.

www.ospreypublishing.com
To find out more about our authors and books visit our website. Here you
will find extracts, author interviews, details of forthcoming events and the
option to sign-up for our newsletter.

ARTIST'S NOTE

Readers may care to note that the original paintings from which
the color plates in this book were prepared are available for private sale.
The Publishers retain all reproduction copyright whatsoever.
All enquiries should be addressed to:

Steve Noon, 50 Colchester Avenue, Penylan, Cardiff, CF23 9BP, UK

The Publishers regret that they can enter into no correspondence
upon this matter.

AUTHOR'S NOTE

The author would like to thank the staff of the US Army's Military History
Institute (MHI) at the Army War College at Carlisle Barracks, PA and the
staff of the US National Archive, College Park for their kind assistance in
the preparation of this book.

For brevity, the traditional conventions have been used when referring
to units. In the case of US units, 2/11th Infantry refers to the 2nd Battalion,
11th Infantry Regiment. The US Army traditionally uses Arabic numerals
for divisions and smaller independent formations (70th Division, 781st Tank
Battalion); Roman numerals for corps (VI Corps), spelled numbers for field
armies (Third Army) and Arabic numerals for army groups (12th Army Group).

In the case of German units, 2./Panzer-Regiment 7 refers to the 2nd
Company, Panzer-Regiment 7; II./Panzer-Regiment 7 indicates 2nd Battalion,
Panzer-Regiment 7. The German field armies are contracted in the usual
fashion (e.g. AOK 1 for First Army).

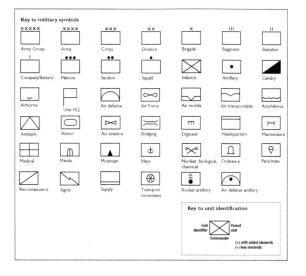

CONTENTS

INTRODUCTION

The Metz campaign by Patton's Third US Army in the late autumn of 1944 is often forgotten or dismissed as a setback. Yet the task faced by his forces in Lorraine in October–December 1944 was amongst his most daunting. The Third US Army had shrunk to only two corps since its glory days in the race to Paris in August 1944, and Patton's units were short of both supplies and fresh troops. Facing them was the most heavily fortified region along the western German frontier, starting with the sturdy 19th-century German forts along the Moselle, followed by a belt of Maginot Line forts, and finally the Westwall pillboxes from the 1930s. In the autumn of 1944, the Wehrmacht modernized and deepened these defensive belts as part of the West-Stellung program. Patton's original attempts to breach the Moselle River on the run in September had mixed results. XII Corps had gained substantial bridgeheads in the areas east of Nancy, but in the XX Corps area Patton had only a small toehold near Metz. The river-crossing sites near Metz were well protected by the neighboring forts and smothered with artillery fire. XX Corps tried to capture Fort Driant in early October 1944, but the attacks failed in the face of fierce resistance. Hitler declared Metz to be a "Festung" (fortress) to be defended to the last bullet.

After a lull in the fighting through most of October dictated by logistics problems, Eisenhower authorized a new round of offensives in early November. Operation *Madison* aimed to reduce Festung Metz but, taking to heart the lessons of the failed Fort Driant attack, intended to infiltrate past the forts where possible and leave them to rot on the vine. The main impediment during the November offensive proved to be the weather. Unusually heavy rains flooded the Moselle Valley, making river-crossing operations especially difficult. In the XII Corps sector, the sodden, muddy conditions turned the battlefield into a quagmire that subverted Patton's usual finesse with tank warfare. In the XX Corps sector, the raging river swept away many bridges, but in the end, the key forts around Thionville were overcome or avoided, and two divisions enveloped Metz. Once the outer crust of forts had been overcome, the city quickly fell on November 18.

In spite of the atrocious weather, Patton's Third US Army managed to overwhelm German forces in Lorraine. By early December, footholds had been secured over the Saar River in the shadows of the Westwall. The ultimate prize was the Rhine River and it seemed to be within their grasp. Operation *Tink* was planned for December 19, 1944, to leap to the Rhine near Mainz and Mannheim in anticipation of a drive on Frankfurt. Days before the launch of this bold winter offensive, the Wehrmacht struck in the Ardennes, diverting Patton's Third US Army northward on its legendary campaign to relieve Bastogne.

CHRONOLOGY

1944

September 5	General der Panzertruppen Otto von Knobelsdorff takes over command of AOK 1 from General der Infanterie Kurt von Chevallerie.
September 7	The 5th Division attempts to cross the Moselle at Dornot, but the bridgehead is overwhelmed by artillery and counterattacks.
September 10	Another 5th Division river crossing at Arnaville proves more successful once a vehicle bridge is erected.
September 21	General der Panzertruppen Hermann Balck takes over command of Heeresgruppe G from Johannes Blaskowitz.
September 22	Eisenhower orders a moratorium on major operations in the Third US Army sector which lasts for six weeks.
September 27	First attack on Fort Driant is repulsed.
October 3	Second attack is launched against Fort Driant, and a toehold secured inside the fort.
October 9	US commanders decide to call off attack on Fort Driant.
October 12–13	Last US troops withdraw from Fort Driant during the night.
October 15	Heeresgruppe G loses 5. Panzerarmee, reducing it to only two field armies for Alsace and Lorraine.
October 20	The 90th Division finally captures the Hôtel de Ville in Maizières-les-Metz.
November 8	Operation *Madison* begins in XII Corps' sector.
November 9	Operation *Madison* begins in XX Corps' sector, starting with a "demonstration" by the 95th Division at Uckange.

November 11	AOK 1 orders the evacuation of non-essential personnel from Metz. Hitler declares the city "Festung Metz" so the city will "fight to the last bullet."
November 14	The 379th Infantry captures three of the "Seven Dwarves" forts: Jussy Nord, Jussy Sud and Saint-Hubert.
November 15	The 378th Infantry captures the Feves Ridge on the night of November 14–15.
November 16	The 11th Infantry pushes into the Luftwaffe's Frescaty airbase near Fort Saint-Privat.
November 17	The last of the Nazi party functionaries leave Metz and French FFI resistance groups begin attacking isolated German troops. At 1900hrs, Generalleutnant Heinrich Kittel orders the demolition of the remaining bridges over the Moselle and Seille rivers.
November 18	US units began entering Metz from numerous directions on November 18. The US divisions began mopping up last pockets of resistance.
November 22	Strasbourg is captured by the Seventh US Army; Heeresgruppe G's two field armies are about to be split apart.
December 3	In a night raid, a battalion of the 95th Division secures a bridge over the Saar in Saarlautern.
December 5	Fort Saint-Quentin surrenders.
December 6	XII Corps wins a toehold in the border town of Sarreguemines.
December 7	Fort Plappeville surrenders.
December 8	Fort Driant surrenders.
December 13	Fort Jeanne d'Arc surrenders.
December 16	German Ardennes offensive begins.
December 17–18	XII Corps operations come to a halt when Third US Army is assigned to relieve Bastogne in the Ardennes.

THE STRATEGIC SETTING

By September 1944, neither Patton's Third US Army, nor its German opponent, 1. Armee, was fighting in the region that their high commands had planned earlier in the summer. The Third US Army had been the follow-on wave after Bradley's First US Army had executed Operation *Cobra*, the breakout from Normandy. Instead of following Bradley's units eastward towards Germany, Patton's forces had been directed westward towards Brittany to seize ports such as Quiberon Bay and Brest. It was a futile mission resulting from the failure of senior Allied commanders to reassess pre-invasion plans. The Germans recognized the Allies' insatiable need for port facilities, and the Wehrmacht demolished ports before their surrender such as Cherbourg in June 1944; there was no reason to expect otherwise at Brest. Furthermore, Brest was hundreds of miles further west of the advancing Allied armies, detracting from its logistical value. Third US Army conducted the Brittany campaign in a speedy fashion, but by mid-August, its futility was evident. Patton convinced Bradley and Eisenhower to redirect his forces eastward towards Paris on Bradley's right flank. It was an ideal mission for

Metz has been fortified since ancient times. The last remnant of the fortified medieval city was the Porte des Allemands (Deutsches Tor) built on the Seille River starting in 1230, and seen here shortly after the end of the fighting in November 1944. (NARA)

The strategic situation, September 25, 1944

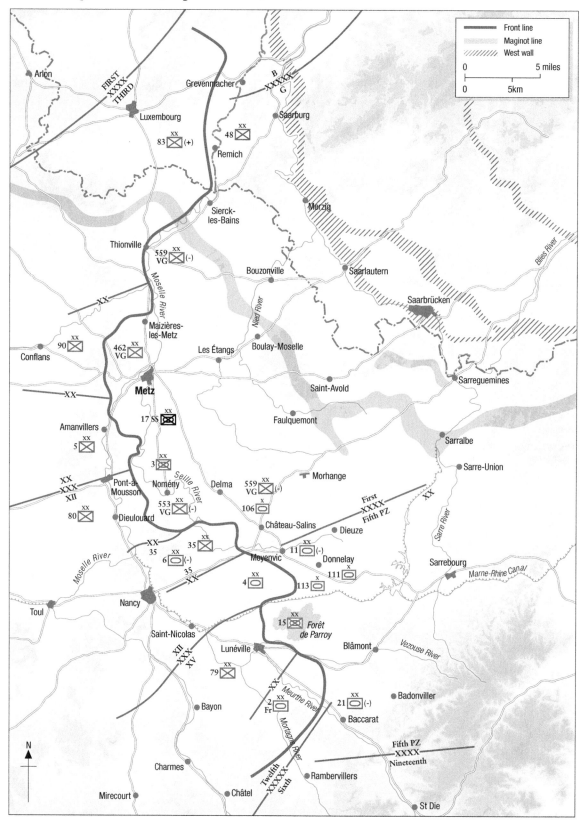

Patton, taking advantage of his skills as a bold cavalry commander on a classic exploitation mission against very weak enemy forces. Patton's spectacular summer advance led to the unexpected liberation of Paris and put the Third US Army on the borders of Lorraine in early September.

The weak forces facing Patton on the approaches to Paris were elements of 1. Armee, better known by its German acronym, AOK 1 (Armeeoberkommando 1). Armeeoberkommando 1 had been assigned the defense of the Atlantic coast from its headquarters in Bordeaux. Its units had been gradually stripped away to reinforce the Normandy front, and by August, it was a shadow of its pre-invasion strength, consisting mainly of third-rate garrison units assigned to coastal defense. When the Wehrmacht in Normandy became trapped in the Falaise pocket, AOK 1 was instructed by Berlin to dispatch a rump headquarters to erect a defensive line in front of Patton's onrushing tanks on the approaches to Paris. It was an impossible mission and one which inevitably failed. Still on the Atlantic coast, the remainder of AOK 1 was in even more desperate circumstances. Operation *Dragoon*, the American and French landings on the French Mediterranean coast on August 15, 1944, succeeded beyond anyone's imagination and Allied forces soon were rushing up the Rhône Valley towards Alsace. Stuck in their Atlantic coastal defenses, AOK 1 was on the verge of being cut off. Uncharacteristically, Hitler

ABOVE LEFT
US troops inspect the ruins of Fort Douaumont on October 1, which had been the infernal center of the Verdun fighting in 1915. Both American and German commanders were skeptical of the value of the old forts under modern battlefield conditions until shown otherwise during the fighting for Fort Driant in early October 1944. (NARA)

ABOVE RIGHT
A motorized column from the 7th Armored Division descends into the Moselle Valley on September 8 on the approaches to Metz. This division took part in the early stages of the Lorraine campaign with XX Corps, but was transferred to the Netherlands later in the month. (NARA)

BOTTOM
The 11th Infantry, 5th Infantry Division, made a crossing of the Moselle in the XX Corps sector near Dornot on September 8. Here a group of infantrymen drag an assault boat to the river. (NARA)

ABOVE LEFT
The initial Moselle crossings by the 5th Infantry Division were resisted by the outer forts of the Mosel-Stellung. Feste Graf Haesler, also known as the Verdun fortified group, was active in bombarding the Dornot River crossing site in early September 1944. The larger of the two forts is Werke St. Blaise (Fort Saint-Blaise) while the smaller is Werke Sommy. (NARA)

ABOVE RIGHT
The vulnerability of the Dornot bridgehead to artillery fire from the forts is evident in this aerial view. The Dornot crossing of the Moselle took place in the center of the lower foreground while the two forts are evident in the background with Fort Saint-Blaise to the left and Fort Sommy to the right. (NARA)

BOTTOM
The scene at Fort Saint-Blaise more than a month later when the troops of the 11th Infantry, 5th Division, raised the American flag following the fort's surrender on November 26. This view clearly shows how the fort overlooked the Moselle Valley below, including the Dornot crossing site. (NARA)

authorized AOK 1 to withdraw along with the rest of Heeresgruppe G (Army Group G) on August 16, 1944. It was a race to see if AOK 1 could reach German lines before the advancing Allied forces could close the trap. Some AOK 1 units reached Lorraine in late August and early September, but on September 10, 1944, Patton's Third US Army linked up from the north with Patch's Seventh US Army from the *Dragoon* force near Dijon, creating a continuous Allied front from the North Sea to the Mediterranean. The final AOK 1 column from the Bordeaux and Biarritz garrisons was trapped on the Loire River, and more than 20,000 troops surrendered on September 15.

Berlin was so alarmed by the rapidity of Patton's advance that a major Panzer counter-blow was planned to stop the Third US Army in Lorraine before it could strengthen its ties with the Seventh US Army. A scratch force was created by hastily deploying new Panzer brigades intended for the Russian Front under the direction of Manteuffel's 5. Panzerarmee. In the event, the counterattack was a shambles, with some of the Panzer units diverted from the attack to plug the gaping holes in German defensive lines in Lorraine, while the rest of the force attacked Patton's XX Corps in a disjointed and ineffective fashion. The Panzer counterattack reached its peak in a series of tank battles near the town of Arracourt on September 19–29, 1944. By the end of September, the fighting ended in stalemate.[1]

1. This campaign is covered in more detail in the author's previous Osprey book Campaign 75: *Lorraine 1944* (Osprey Publishing Ltd: Oxford, 2000)

TOP
The Arnaville bridgehead proved to be more successful after the engineers were able to erect a pontoon treadway bridge over the Moselle. In addition, the site was shielded from observation of nearby Fort Driant and the Verdun fortified group by smoke generators as seen here on September 23. (NARA)

BOTTOM
XII Corps made numerous crossings of the Moselle in the Nancy area in September. An M4A3 tank and Jagdpanzer IV are seen here at a crossroads on the eastern bank of the Moselle near Dieulouard where the 80th Division, supported by elements of the 4th Armored Division, fought off a major counterattack by the 3. Panzergrenadier-Division in mid-September 1944. (NARA)

Compared with the XX Corps in the Nancy area, the neighboring XII Corps to the north facing Metz had far less success in September in breaching the Moselle barrier. The 5th Infantry Division staged an initial bridging attempt near Dornot on September 7, but the bridgehead was quickly smothered by artillery fire from nearby forts including Fort Driant and the Verdun fortification group. A second bridgehead secured near Arnaville starting on September 10 proved to be more durable once a vehicle bridge was erected.

By the end of September, Patton's Third US Army had been halted by the logistical problems affecting the entire Allied front. The rapid Allied breakout from Normandy had exhausted fuel supplies and units were located far deeper into France and Belgium than had been anticipated. Until the logistical situation could be remedied, on September 22, Eisenhower ordered Allied forces to halt and await further instructions. There was a six-week lull in most Allied ground operations through early November 1944.

In the German case, the Arracourt battles east of Nancy had exhausted what few reserves were immediately on hand, and German formations on the western front were in a desperate state after the summer defeats. Armeeoberkommando 1 had to create new defenses in Lorraine with minimal forces. The one asset in AOK 1's favor was the extensive array of defensive fortifications in Lorraine.

Feste Obergentringen was part of the Diedenhofen (Thionville) fortification belt built in the 1890s and located on the west bank of the Moselle in support of Feste Königsmacker and Feste Illingen. After World War I, the French army absorbed it into the Maginot Line as Fort de Guentrange and replaced the original short 105mm howitzer tubes in its Panzerbatterien with the longer ones seen here. These armored cupolas are typical of the Schumann turrets used in other Metz–Diedenhofen forts such as Fort Driant. The fort was captured by the 358th Infantry, 90th Division, without a fight on September 12, 1944. The gun turrets were reoriented eastward to assist in combat operations towards Thionville and are seen firing on October 2, 1944. Today, the fort is the site of a museum. (NARA)

Lorraine (Lothringen) had been a traditional warpath between France and Germany over the past millennia. The city of Metz was sacked by Attila the Hun in April AD 451, the last time the city was taken by storm. In the contemporary era, the province has been a bone of contention between France and Germany, with Germany coveting Lorraine as a means to shield the Saar region by preventing access into central Germany via the "Moselle Gate." In the wake of the 1870 Franco-Prussian War, Lorraine became part of the Reich.

The Moselle River valley took on considerable importance in German war planning since a well-fortified Metz–Diedenhofen barrier could act as a pivot for German forces advancing into northern France through Belgium. As a result, the Mosel-Stellung (Moselle Line) was constructed in the Moselle Valley from Metz to Diedenhofen (Thionville) in the last decades of the 19th century to serve this strategic objective.[2] It served this function well in the First World War, shielding the Moselle Gate and allowing the execution of the Schlieffen Plan in 1914. In the wake of the war, Lorraine returned to France and the Mosel-Stellung fell into neglect. Instead, the French built a portion of the Maginot Line in Lorraine further east along the German frontier. Following the rise to power of Hitler in the 1930s, German strategic planners again sought to use this region as a fortified pivot point for further operations into France down the Belgian corridor. As a result, the Westwall fortification line constructed in the Saar opposite Lorraine was especially dense. With its purpose served, the Westwall fell into disrepair following the defeat of France in 1940. Nevertheless, the paucity of forces available to AOK 1 led to a rejuvenation of the old fortification lines as well as the construction of an extensive network of new field fortifications under the West-Stellung (West-Position) program.[3] Many senior German commanders were skeptical of the value of the old and forgotten Mosel-Stellung forts around Metz, and it took the initiative of local junior commanders to show them the intrinsic tactical value of these forts even in an age of mechanized warfare.

2. For further details see Clayton Donnell, Fortress 78: *The German Fortress of Metz 1870–1944* (Osprey Publishing Ltd: Oxford, 2008)

3. For further details see Steven Zaloga, Fortress 102: *The Defense of the Rhine 1944–45* (Osprey Publishing Ltd: Oxford, 2011)

OPPOSING COMMANDERS

AMERICAN COMMANDERS

Lieutenant-General George S. Patton was one of the most famous American commanders of World War II both for his military accomplishments and his colorful personality. He served with Pershing's expeditionary force in Mexico in 1916, and commanded the first American Expeditionary Force tank battalions in France in 1918 before being wounded. He was given command of the 2nd Armored Division in 1940, and, shortly before America's entry into the war in 1941, Patton was again promoted to lead I Armored Corps. He led the Western Task Force landings in French North Africa in November 1942 as part of Operation *Torch*. After the Kasserine Pass debacle in February 1943, Patton was reassigned to lead II Corps and he helped redeem the honor of the US Army with its first tactical victory against the Wehrmacht at El Guettar in March 1943. He was assigned to command the Seventh US Army for Operation *Husky*, the amphibious assault on Sicily in July 1943. Even though the US Army was assigned a secondary role in the offensive actions on Sicily, Patton's aggressive determination pushed the US units to Palermo, setting the stage for the concluding capture of Messina after the neighboring British advance bogged down. Patton's fortunes ebbed in late 1943 as the result of his rash behavior when it became public that he had slapped two shell-shocked soldiers. This scandal nearly derailed Patton's career, but Eisenhower valued Patton's skill with mechanized formations and assigned him to command the Third US Army.

At the time of Operation *Madison* in early November 1944, the Third US Army had shrunk down to only two corps (XII and XX) with a third (III Corps) in the process of formation. **Major-General Manton S. Eddy** commanded XII Corps. He was a considerable contrast to Patton, a cautious infantryman to the bone. He had been commissioned in the Army in 1916 from a small military academy and not West Point, served in infantry units in World War I, and after the war served in a variety of posts including as a tactics instructor at the Command and General Staff School. Compared with other corps commanders, he had not been groomed for higher command and had not attended the Army War College. At the beginning of the war, he was an infantry regiment commander and, during the Tunisia campaign, he commanded the 9th Infantry Division. Although the division got off to a rocky start, Eddy soon developed a reputation as a solid commander and came to Patton's attention for his actions both in Tunisia and Sicily. Eddy was

transferred to head XII Corps on August 19, 1944, when Major-General Gilbert "Doc" Cook was relieved for medical reasons. Under Eddy's command, the corps became known as "the Spearhead of Patton's Third Army." It tended to be an armor-heavy formation, including both the 4th and 6th Armored Divisions during most of the summer and autumn campaigns. During the explosive breakout from Normandy, it was XII Corps that raced to the Seine. Eddy found Patton's daring tactical style a bit uncomfortable. In Normandy, his infantry division had been bitterly battling their way through the hedgerows yards at a time; a mile a day was good progress. When given command of XII Corps, Patton told him his day's objective was 50 miles behind German lines. He was uncomfortable about advancing so far, so fast with exposed flanks, but Patton told him to ignore the flanks. Unaccustomed to bold cavalry tactics carried out by armored divisions, Eddy soon came to trust Patton's judgments and to accommodate himself to the new style of war. Nevertheless, his infantryman's perspective would cause tensions with both Patton and his subordinate armored division commanders, most notably with John "Tiger Jack" Wood of the 4th Armored Division. Eddy was well liked by his troops; the legendary journalist Ernie Pyle dubbed him "Old Shoe."

Major-General Walton Walker who commanded XX Corps was much closer in temperament to Patton. He was nicknamed "Johnnie" as in Johnnie Walker scotch, or "Bulldog" owing to his fierce pug appearance. Patton dubbed him "my fightingest son-of-a-bitch." Walker was a graduate of West Point, class of 1912, and served on the Mexican border in 1916. He was decorated with the Silver Star for gallantry as an infantry officer in France in 1918. During the interwar years he served in a variety of infantry posts but when the Armored Force was formed in 1940, Walker lobbied Marshall for a transfer to the new branch. He became commander of the 3rd Armored Division in 1942, and later took over IV Armored Corps, which was redesignated XX Corps in October 1943. Like Patton, he was an energetic, hands-on commander who could usually be found speeding around the front lines by jeep to prod his divisional commanders forward. XX Corps became nicknamed "the Ghost Corps" after a German prisoner of war called Walker's corps by that name in an interrogation because the corps had moved so fast and so often that the Wehrmacht had been unable to keep track of them.

GERMAN COMMANDERS

AOK 1 was part of Heeresgruppe G, which in the autumn of 1944, consisted of three field armies, AOK 1 and 5. Panzerarmee in Lorraine, and AOK 19 in Alsace. On October 15, 1944, 5. Panzerarmee was withdrawn into Germany to refit for the planned Ardennes offensive, leaving Heeresgruppe G with only two field armies to cover the entire Alsace-Lorraine front.

Heeresgruppe G had been commanded by Generaloberst Johannes Blaskowitz who was relieved on September 21 because of Hitler's displeasure over the high cost of the retreat from southern and central France and the failure of the Lorraine Panzer counterattack. He was replaced by **General der Panzertruppen Hermann Balck** who had been commanding 4. Panzerarmee on the Russian Front. Balck was one of the best-known Russian Front Panzer commanders and he had been elevated from corps to army command at the beginning of August 1944. His rise was unusually rapid and part of Hitler's effort to reinvigorate key command positions in the west with an infusion of young blood from the east. In the event, Balck's command of Heeresgruppe G would be short lived after AOK 1 and 19 were comprehensively smashed in the November–December 1944 fighting. Blaskowitz was called back to command on December 23 in the hopes of providing a steady hand after the autumn disasters.

Armeeoberkommando 1 had been commanded for most of the summer of 1944 by General der Infanterie Kurt von Chevallerie. He was relieved on September 5, 1944, because of Berlin's dissatisfaction with his handling of the defense along the Seine. Command was transferred to **General der Panzertruppen Otto von Knobelsdorff**, another distinguished Russian Front Panzer veteran. During the Great War, he served as an infantry officer, was decorated twice with the Iron Cross for bravery, and was severely wounded in October 1918. He served in the Reichswehr after the war, commanding an infantry regiment in 1935, and serving as chief of staff of XXXIII AK in the Polish Campaign at the start of World War II. Knobelsdorff commanded the 19. Infanterie-Division in the campaign for France in 1940, fighting against the British Expeditionary Force (BEF) in Belgium. In October 1940, the division was reorganized as the 19. Panzer-Division, and he led this division during the invasion of Russia in 1941. He was decorated with the Knight's Cross on September 17, 1941, for his division's performance in Russia and, in May–October 1942, served as a corps commander on the northern front

in Russia. He was promoted to General der Panzertruppen on August 1, 1942, and he again distinguished himself as a Panzer corps commander in the attempts to relieve Stalingrad. He remained a Panzer corps commander through September 1944, being decorated again on November 12, 1943, for his leadership of XLVIII Panzer Korps during the battle of Kursk with the Knight's Cross with Oakleaves, and, in September 1944, for his leadership of the XL Panzer Korps in the Nikopol bridgehead with Oakleaves and Sword. In spite of his exemplary record, there was some concern in Berlin over his appointment to AOK 1 in Lorraine because of the heavy toll on his health from the battles on the Russian Front; he had been temporarily relieved on two occasions in 1942 and 1943 because of serious illnesses. This indeed proved the case, as at the beginning of November, Knobelsdorff's health had deteriorated to the point where he was sent on furlough for several weeks during the height of the battle. **General der Infanterie Kurt von Tippelskirch** was brought to the headquarters at Saint-Avold on October 31, nominally as Knobelsdorff's deputy, but acting as the temporary army commander through November 11, 1944. Tippelskirch was an experienced staff officer with combat tours on the Russian and Italian fronts, and had been acting commander of AOK 4 on the Russian front earlier in the summer.

At the time of Operation *Madison* in November 1944, AOK 1 had three subordinate corps. The northern flank was covered by LXXXII AK commanded by **General der Infanterie Walter Hörnlein**. He started the war as an infantry battalion commander, winning the Iron Cross and being decorated again in the summer of 1941 for his leadership of the 80. Infanterie-Regiment in Russia. He commanded the famous Großdeutschland Division from April 1942 to February 1944, being decorated with the German Cross in Gold in February 1943 and the Knight's Cross with Oakleaves in March 1943.

The XIII SS-Korps was commanded initially by **SS-Gruppenführer Hermann Preiss**, but he was selected to lead the spearhead I SS-Panzer-Korps in the forthcoming Ardennes offensive, so his place was taken by **SS-Gruppenführer Max Simon**. He had served in World War I where he won the Iron Cross, and fought with the Freikorps in Silesia in the ensuing turmoil. He was an NCO in the postwar Reichswehr, becoming a Nazi Party and SS member in 1933. In 1934, he was appointed commander of the Sachsenburg concentration camp. He commanded the 1. SS-Panzergrenadier-Regiment "Totenkopf" during the 1940 campaign in France, and subsequently in the invasion of Russia in 1941. Decorated with the Knight's Cross after the battle for the Demyansk Pocket, he was promoted to *Brigadeführer* and transferred to command the 16. SS-Panzergrenadier-Division "Reichsführer-SS" being formed in Hungary. This incomplete division was sent to Italy in July 1944 where it became involved in a number of anti-partisan operations for which the Allies would later convict Simon for war crimes. He was awarded the Oakleaves to his Knight's Cross for his actions in Italy and promoted *Gruppenführer* in November 1944.

The southern corps, LXXXIX AK, was commanded by **General der Infanterie Werner von und zu Gilsa**. Like the other commanders, he was a decorated veteran of World War I, twice recipient of the Iron Cross, and served in the postwar Reichswehr as a young captain. He commanded the 9. Infanterie-Regiment since 1936 and led it during the campaign in Poland in 1939, being decorated twice again with the Iron Cross for leadership. His regiment captured Charleville and several Maas (Meuse) bridges in the 1940 campaign, and by the start of the war in Russia, Gilsa commanded the 216. Infanterie-Division. He was decorated with the Knight's Cross in June 1940 and with Oakleaves in January 1942. He took command of LXXXIX AK in June 1943, and led it during the defense of the Scheldt in the Netherlands in October 1944 before the headquarters was transferred to Lorraine. He later served as the commandant of Dresden at the time of the fire-bombing attacks in 1945.

The commander of Festung Driant was Hauptmann August Weiler, an instructor at the Fahnenjunkerschule VI Metz, and commander of Lehrgang 3 of Kampfgruppe Stössel during the Moselle fighting in September 1944. He was awarded the Knight's Cross for his leadership at Fort Driant, but rather than take his allotted 21-day leave, he remained in Metz to take part in the defense and was captured during the street fighting there in November. (NARA)

OPPOSING FORCES

US ARMY

Walker's XX Corps at the time of Operation *Madison* had three infantry and one armored divisions. The armor contingent was reinforced by seven tank destroyer battalions (two attached to divisions) and three separate tank battalions (all attached to divisions). Corps artillery was quite substantial totaling some 19 battalions (five light, six medium, and eight heavy) plus a further two artillery battalions from an artillery group attached to the uncommitted 83rd Division. The 83rd Division had been begrudgingly allotted to Walker's control under Eisenhower's instructions, but Bradley wanted it back further north and so it did not participate in Operation *Madison* beyond the use of its artillery. In total, XX Corps had 30 infantry battalions, 373 M4 medium tanks, 171 M5A1 light tanks, and over 700 field guns at the start of the offensive.

The unusually wet autumn in Lorraine limited mechanized operations to "a front one tank wide." A partial solution to the pervasive autumn mud was to attach extenders to the track end connectors, and these can be seen on this tank from C/69th Tank Battalion, 6th Armored Division. These were given various nicknames by the troops such as "duck bills" or "duck feet." (NARA)

Eddy's XII Corps to the south was the armor-heavy portion of the Third US Army, with two armored divisions and three infantry divisions as well as three separate tank battalions and seven tank destroyer battalions. Tank strength at the start of Operation *Madison* was 567 medium and 273 light tanks. The corps had substantial firepower including 17 field artillery battalions besides the divisional battalions, and it was reinforced with a few battalions from the neighboring XX Corps sector when the attack was launched on November 8.

The US divisions took advantage of the October lull to rebuild strength after the heavy infantry losses in the August–September fighting. The Third US Army was especially short of artillery ammunition because of the priority afforded to gasoline in the August–September race to Lorraine. As a result, artillery preparation of German targets before the start of Operation *Madison* was severely limited. Curiously enough, the majority of artillery ammunition fired by the Third US Army in late October were captured German rounds, often from captured German guns.

Patton had learned from wargames in the US in 1940–41 of the absolute necessity of tactical bridging in offensive operations, and he took great pains to build up his engineer forces and to bolster the stock of assault boats, treadway bridging and other engineer equipment. This would prove absolutely essential in the November Lorraine attack because of the need to bridge the Moselle in the Thionville sector and the unanticipated need for more bridging and engineer equipment to cope with the extensive flooding.

Air support for the Lorraine offensive was limited both by the low priority afforded to the Third US Army as well as the weather. Medium bombers were seldom available, and most air support came from P-47 Thunderbolt fighters. The rainy weather and low cloud cover severely limited the amount of air support available.

THIRD US ARMY

Lt. Gen. George S. Patton Jr.

XII CORPS

Maj. Gen. Manton Eddy

26th Division

Maj. Gen. Willard Paul

    101 IR

    104 IR

    328 IR

35th Division

Maj. Gen. Paul Baade

    134 IR

    137 IR

    320 IR

80th Division

Maj. Gen. Horace McBride

    317 IR

    318 IR

    319 IR

4th Armored Division

Maj. Gen. John Wood

    8 TB

    35 TB

    37 TB

    10 AIB

    51 AIB

    53 AIB

6th Armored Division

Maj. Gen. Robert Grow

    15 TB

    68 TB

    69 TB

    9 AIB

    44 AIB

    50 AIB

XX CORPS

Maj. Gen. Walton Walker

5th Infantry Division

Maj. Gen. LeRoy Irwin

    2 IR

    10 IR

    11 IR

90th Division

Maj. Gen. Raymond McClain

    357 IR

    358 IR

    359 IR

95th Division

Maj. Gen. Harry Twaddle

    377 IR

    378 IR

    379 IR

10th Armored Division

Maj. Gen. William Morris

    3 TB

    11 TB

    21 TB

    20 AIB

    54 AIB

    61 AIB

AIB – Armored Infantry Battalion

IR – Infantry Regiment

TB – Tank Battalion

GERMAN ARMY

Hitler's decision in the autumn of 1944 to stage a counteroffensive in the Ardennes late in the year inevitably meant that other sectors would be reduced to a starvation diet of replacements and fresh units. The size of German forces in Lorraine shrank during the October 1944 lull. Manteuffel's 5. Panzerarmee was withdrawn on October 15 to permit rebuilding for the Ardennes attack, and the southern sector of the Lorraine front had to be taken over by AOK 1, substantially increasing the frontage it had to cover. Besides the withdrawal of Manteuffel's headquarters, there was considerable shifting of corps headquarters and boundaries during this period, and the chart here reflects the organization at the beginning of November in the days before the start of Operation *Madison*. The heavy losses in the September Lorraine fighting and the transfer of the 5. Panzerarmee drastically reduced

LEFT
Two unit commanders of a Volksgrenadier division study a map during the fighting in Lorraine in November 1944. The *Feldwebel* (sergeant) to the left is armed with a Sturmgewehr 44 assault rifle, a new type specifically earmarked for the Volksgrenadier units. Behind him, the infantryman is carrying a Panzerfaust anti-tank rocket. (NARA)

RIGHT
By the late autumn, the supply of Luftwaffe and Kriegsmarine personnel had gone dry and the Wehrkreis became reliant on less satisfactory sources of troops, particularly young boys and old men. These Volkssturm troops were captured during the fighting in Saarlautern in mid-December 1944, led by the *Kompanieführer* (Captain) seen here wearing the Volkssturm armband. (NARA)

the number of armored vehicles available in this sector. Nearly 700 tanks and medium AFVs had been committed to the Lorraine counterattack in mid-September, but by the end of October, this had been reduced to only about 85. Armeeoberkommando 1 deployed 86,622 troops on November 1, 1944, less than half the strength of Patton's Third Army. In spite of this significant

The "miracle on the Westwall" was made possible by the sudden infusion of Luftwaffe and Kriegsmarine personnel into the infantry divisions in September 1944 because of the fuel shortages that left so many aircraft and warships idle. The section seen advancing here was made up of Kriegsmarine personnel; the nearest soldier is armed with an obsolete 7.92mm MG13, a type largely replaced by the better-known MG34. (Library of Congress)

Armeeoberkommando 1 was relatively weak in armor with the badly weakened 11. Panzer-Division its only major reserve at the start of the Operation *Madison* offensive in November 1944. The division was committed in the XII Corps sector owing to the mistaken belief that this was the main focus of the American attack. This Jagdpanzer IV of 11. Panzer-Division was knocked out by the 6th Armored Division near Saint-Jean Rohrbach on November 25, 1944, with its mantlet blown off and evidence of a hit on the right side of the casemate. (NARA)

cutback in forces, AOK 1 enjoyed some less obvious advantages because of its proximity to the Reich and the resources available in the military district to its rear, Wehrkreis XII. Although AOK 1 was significantly smaller than the Third US Army, the rear area military districts continued to feed in infantry battalions and replacements through the course of the campaign.

In early November 1944, AOK 1 bore little resemblance to the original formation that had been deployed on the Atlantic coast in the summer of 1944. Most of its original units had been captured or had disintegrated during the retreat. When the AOK 1 headquarters arrived in Lorraine in early September, the task was mainly to create a new defensive line using whatever forces were available. Two of its corps headquarters had been stationed on the Atlantic Wall in the summer of 1944. LXXXII AK controlled one of the high-priority sectors of the anti-invasion defenses on the Pas-de-Calais, but after this area was bypassed by the Normandy battles, the headquarters was shifted deeper into France as part of the effort to defend the Seine and later the Moselle. By early September 1944, LXXXII AK controlled the northern shoulder of the AOK 1 sector, headquartered at Fremersdorf. LXXXIX AK had been stationed on the Scheldt Estuary and took part in the initial fighting against British and Canadian forces in the late summer of 1944 before being extracted in October. It was first stationed on the northern shoulder of AOK 19 near Dompaire in late October until taking over the previous LVIII AK headquarters at Les Bachats on November 1, 1944, on the southern flank of AOK 1. The XIII SS AK was a new formation created in Breslau in the summer of 1944. It arrived in Lorraine in September 1944, originally headquartered at Bolchen. This headquarters was only partly formed on its arrival in Lorraine, lacking requisite signals troops, but it was built up to strength during October because it was considered the focal point (*Schwerpunkt*) of the AOK 1 defenses.

When AOK 1 retreated into Lorraine in September 1944, it deployed a ragged skeleton force along the Moselle. Aside from remnants of the units originally defending the Seine, the Moselle front was covered by a number of ad hoc formations that had been pushed forward by the Wehrkreis XII military district. Metz was defended originally by a collection of school units which might seem unimpressive on first glance, but which proved to be an extremely capable force due to the high quality of the troops involved. The core of the force, sometimes called Kampfgruppe Stössel, was the Metz officer candidate's school (Fahnenjunkerschule VI Metz) numbering about 1,500 troops. Several other schools also contributed troops including the army NCO school (Heeres-Unteroffizier Schule Bergzabern), an SS signals school (SS-Nachrichten Schule Metz), and the military district NCO training regiment (Wehrkreis Unteroffizier Lehrregiment XII). Four local border guard (*Zollgrenzschutzen*) companies were added to this force, bringing its strength to 3,500 troops. Many of these units were expended in the fighting along the Moselle in September 1944, and in early October, there was an effort made to pull out the officer cadets and send them to their command assignments on the Russian Front.

During the lull in mid-October after the first battle for Fort Driant, the Festung Metz defense force was more formally organized. The Metz replacement division, called variously 462. Ausbildungs-Division or Division 462, was a skeleton formation with only two infantry training battalions and a machine-gun training unit. This served as the organizational basis for the new 462. Volksgrenadier-Division created on October 19, 1944. The scattered elements of the Metz defense force formed two of its regiments while the Sicherungs-Regiment 1010 became its third. The division was finally renamed as Festungs-Division "Metz" in the final weeks of combat.

Of AOK 1's eight infantry divisions, five were newly formed Volksgrenadier divisions. These divisions were a new alternative to conventional infantry divisions. The new configuration was intended to offer maximum firepower with minimum personnel and equipment. They were originally called defense divisions (*Sperrdivisionen*) and were intended for defensive missions on elongated fronts, and so not optimized for offensive missions because of inadequate mobile resources. To cut down on personnel, the infantry component took one of two forms, either a three-regiment configuration with a reduced regimental strength of only two grenadier battalions each, or a two-regiment configuration with the normal three battalions. In either case, the new organization proved awkward in combat since in the case of the common two-battalion regiment, it compelled the commander to keep both battalions in the line instead of the usual practice of leaving one battalion free as a reserve or for rest and re-equipping. The Volksgrenadier units were supposed to be favored in the appointment of regimental and battalion commanders and assigned young, combat-proven officers with a minimum of the German Cross in Gold, and preferably holders of the Knight's Cross or Iron Cross. This often proved impossible because of shortages. To make up for its weakened force structure, one or two platoons in each rifle company were supposed to be armed with the Sturmgewehr 43 assault rifle instead of the standard 98k rifle. To enhance anti-tank defense, the units were equipped with large numbers of Panzerfaust anti-tank rockets. Efforts were also made to equip each division with a company of 14 Jagdpanzer 38(t) Hetzer or StuG III assault guns, but few of the divisions in Lorraine in the autumn of 1944 had any of these. The 19. Volksgrenadier-Division received 11 assault guns shortly before the November fighting.

The other three infantry divisions in AOK 1 were of very mixed quality. The best equipped was the 17. SS-Panzergrenadier-Division "Gotz von Berlichingen." However, the division had been short of officers ever since its deployment in France in the summer of 1944, and it was so badly beaten up in the fighting with the US Army in Normandy that it had to be rebuilt and reorganized in the Metz area in late August 1944. Some of its regiments were decimated again in the fighting along the Moselle. Its nominal composition as a Panzergrenadier division was undermined by lingering shortages of armored vehicles and half-tracks, with only a handful of StuG IV assault guns on hand. It was amply equipped with new troops, but the AOK 1 staff was unhappy with its dependence on *Volksdeutsche* recruits, ethnic Germans from Hungary and Yugoslavia, who the army staff felt "could not be depended upon for one moment." The army staff rated the division as having limited suitability for defense.

The 48. Infanterie-Division had been formed in the summer of 1944 from the 171. Reserve-Division in Belgium and had been part of the AOK 1 battlegroup that had tried to stop Patton's advance on the Seine in August 1944 in the Chartres area. The division lost most of its combat strength in the fighting and was sent back to the Trier region for rebuilding. The 416. Infanterie-Division was another makeshift creation that had been stationed in Denmark for garrison duty until October 4, 1944. It consisted of two fortress infantry regiments that lost four *Ostruppen* (Russian) battalions during the transfer; its third regiment was added on arrival in Lorraine. The division was made up of troops mostly over 40 years old and it was often called a "whipped-cream" (*Schlagsahne*) division because many of its troops had stomach problems and were allotted a special diet.

The best unit under AOK 1 command was the 11. Panzer-Division, which was pulled off the line from the fighting around Dieuze on October 28 and given a few weeks to rebuild. This division had been in continual combat with the US Army since the Operation *Dragoon* amphibious landings on the Riviera coast. The division distinguished itself by its exemplary rearguard actions for Heeresgruppe G during the retreat up the Rhône Valley. During late September and early October, the division was heavily involved in the fighting to contain Third US Army around Parroy. It had been reduced to 18 PzKpfw IV and 20 Panther tanks by the end of October 1944. The division

received a few replacement tanks and some personnel in early November, bringing its strength up to about 20 PzKpfw IV, 40 Panther tanks and about ten Panzerjäger IV tank destroyers.

In spite of the paltry AOK 1 order of battle, the German defenses in Lorraine benefited from the extensive defensive works in this area. Due to its recent history, Lorraine was the site of a deep series of fortified defenses, created over the past century to defend this traditional invasion route between France and Germany. These fortifications had been neglected since 1940 and some had been stripped of equipment, weapons, and other components in 1942–44 to help in the construction of the Atlantikwall anti-invasion defenses. Recognizing the derelict state of the border defenses, Hitler issued Führer Directive Nr. 61 on August 24, 1944, starting the new West-Stellung (West Position) program. The instructions authorized a rejuvenation of the Westwall defenses, incorporation of suitable sections of the Maginot Line into the German border defenses, and the addition of new lines of fieldworks and fortifications. Hitler singled out the Metz–Diedenhofen sector for special attention as he intended to use this sector in its traditional strategic fashion as a solid pivot to allow the unfettered advance of German forces into the Ardennes in December.

The Mosel-Stellung fortifications had been created after Lorraine was absorbed into the Reich following the 1870 Franco-Prussian war. Although formidable by late 19th-century standards, the fortifications were made of normal concrete and earth, and not steel-reinforced concrete comparable to the Maginot Line or Westwall. They had been modernized prior to World War I with *Panzerbatterien* for their principal guns. By 1944, there was some skepticism about their defensive value, but surveys by the Metz officer cadets in early October determined that a significant number of gun turrets were still operable, ammunition was still available, and the design of the forts was well suited to anti-tank defense. The primary tactical role of the Metz fortification belt was to dominate the nearby Moselle Valley and prevent river crossings by means of heavy artillery fire. A desperate program of rejuvenation was undertaken during the October lull in fighting. This consisted of reactivating the forts by locating ammunition, gun sights, and firing tables. In addition, the defenses were improved by the addition of fieldworks.

LEFT
An RSO (Raupenschlepper Ost) tractor of 2./Artillerie-Regiment 719 of the 19. Volksgrenadier-Division captured by the US Army during the fighting near Sierk-les-Bains in late November 1944. These prime movers were used to tow the standard 105mm field gun and this particular vehicle was assigned to the 5. Batterie as is evident from its markings. (NARA)

RIGHT
The West-Stellung program in Lorraine aimed at incorporating the old Maginot Line and Mosel-Stellung forts and amplifying the defenses with new field works like this anti-tank ditch erected near Sierk-les-Bains to the north of Thionville. A Maginot Line fort is evident on the hill in the background. (NARA)

Aside from the initial efforts by the officer cadets, the new fortification effort in Lorraine was undertaken primarily by rear elements of the army based in Germany, and not by tactical combat formations. Lorraine was the responsibility of the Höheres Kommando Saarpfalz (Saar-Palatinate High Command) headquartered in Landstuhl. The defense sector in Lorraine was managed by Festungs-Pionier-Kommandeur IV (Fortification Engineer Command IV). This headquarters planned the fortification effort and coordinated work between army front-line units, rear support commands and Nazi Party district leaders (*Gauleiter*) as well as the paramilitary Organization Todt construction agency. To facilitate the creation of fieldworks, the *Gauleiter* were instructed to call up hundreds of thousands of local civilians to assist in digging trenches and other field fortifications under the direction of army engineers. There were more construction workers building the Lorraine defenses in the early autumn of 1944 than there were troops in AOK 1. By mid-September 1944, there were nearly 80,000 workers constructing fortifications in Lorraine, and they had already completed 22 miles (35km) of anti-tank ditches, 16 miles (26km) of reinforced trenches, 277 machine-gun nests, 153 anti-tank gun pits, and six emplaced tank turrets. Heeresgruppe G singled out two areas for special priority for mines, the Belfort Gap in Alsace in the AOK 19 sector and the Thionville sector north of Metz in the AOK 1 sector. As a result, the garrison at Thionville was issued 40,000 mines, emplaced by special engineer units.

Aside from the construction of new defensive lines and the rejuvenation of the existing fortifications, the West-Stellung program also involved the reinforcement of the front lines with additional weapons collected from depots in neighboring German districts, and the deployment of specialized fortification (*Festung*) units. This type of formation had largely disappeared from the German order of battle after 1940, but they were resurrected in the late summer of 1944 owing to the rejuvenation of the Westwall. These included infantry (*Festung-Infanterie-Bataillon*), machine gun (*Festung-MG-Bataillon*), light Flak (*Festung-schwere-MG-Bataillon*), and artillery (*Festung-Artillerie-Abteilung*). These were primarily intended to man the Westwall defenses, but in the autumn of 1944, many of these units were pushed forward to help reinforce the Mosel-Stellung. Wehrkreis XII deployed seven fortification infantry battalions, nine MG battalions and light Flak battalions armed with 398 light MG, 366 heavy MG, 255 50mm mortars, 180 20mm Flak and 54 37mm Flak guns. Wehrkreis XII had an extensive if somewhat motley selection of field artillery to supplement the artillery of AOK 1 totaling some 379 field guns ranging from World War I 77mm field guns to 305mm siege mortars. There were also a half-dozen large-caliber railway guns in Eisenbahn-Artillerie Abteilung 640.

Although Festungs-Pionier-Kommandeur IV in Lorraine was near full strength in machine guns and mortars for its associated fortifications, it lacked anti-tank guns at the beginning of October. The West-Stellung program planned to add new anti-tank battalions (*Festung-PaK-Abteilungen*) using surplus tank guns mounted on improvised fixed pedestal mounts. However, these were not yet ready in sufficient numbers so the units deployed in Lorraine were equipped with 36 normal 75mm PaK 40 towed anti-tank guns, 32 88mm PaK 43, 96 captured Russian 76mm field guns and 42 88mm Flak guns in an anti-tank role.

The Luftwaffe would not provide much support to the army in the ensuing battles. At the beginning of September, Jagdkorps II had about 420 fighters and fighter-bombers, of which about 110 covered the Nancy–Metz area of Lorraine. The bomber force was largely grounded because of fuel shortages. US aircraft encountered the Luftwaffe in large numbers on only two occasions during the Lorraine fighting in September, and found that the pilots were inexperienced due to the heavy summer losses and the priority given to the air defense of the Reich.

1. ARMEE (AOK 1)
Gen. der Panzertruppen Hermann Balck

11. Panzer-Division
Gen.Lt. Wend von Wietersheim
>   PzRgt 15
>   PGR 4
>   PGR 110

559. Volksgrenadier-Division
Gen.Lt. Kurt von Mühlen
>   VGR 1125
>   VGR 1126
>   VGR 1127

LXXXII AK
Gen. der Inf. Walter Hörnlein

416. Infanterie-Division
Gen.Lt. Kurt Pfleiger
>   GR 712
>   GR 713
>   GR 714

19. Volksgrenadier-Division
Gen.Lt. Walter Wißmath
>   VGR 59
>   VGR 73
>   VGR 74

462. Volksgrenadier-Division
Gen.Lt. Heinrich Kittel
>   VGR 1010
>   VGR 1215
>   VGR 1216

LXXXIX AK
Gen. der Inf. Werner von und zu Gilsa

361. Volksgrenadier-Division
Gen.Maj. Alfred Philippi
>   VGR 951
>   VGR 952
>   VGR 953

553. Volksgrenadier-Division
Gen.Maj. Hans Bruhn
>   VGR 1119
>   VGR 1120

GR – Grenadier Regiment
PzBn – Panzer Battalion
PzRgt – Panzer Regiment
PGR – Panzergrenadier Regiment
VGR – Volksgrenadier Regiment

XIII SS-KORPS
SS-Gruppenführer Max Simon

17. SS-Panzergrenadier-Division
Brigadeführer Werner Ostendorff
>   SS-PzBn 17
>   SS-PGR 37
>   SS-PGR 38

48. Infanterie-Division
Gen.Maj. Gerhard Kegler
>   VGR 126
>   VGR 127
>   VGR 128

OPPOSING PLANS

AMERICAN PLANS

Operations in Lorraine during the autumn of 1944 were heavily shaped by the logistics problems facing the Allies since the rapid advance of August–September 1944. On September 11, 1944, the first day US troops entered Germany near Aachen, the Allies were along a phase line that the Operation *Overlord* plans did not expect to reach until D+330, May 2, 1945, some 233 days ahead of schedule. Allied logistics had not yet caught up with the pace of the advance, and on September 22, Eisenhower's SHAEF (Supreme Headquarters Allied Expeditionary Force) ordered a moratorium of operations until further notice.

SHAEF's primary operational objective in the autumn of 1944 was to open the port of Antwerp to provide an essential logistics hub for the forthcoming campaign into Germany. The port had already been taken in September 1944, but it could not be used until the Scheldt Estuary leading to

At the 5th Infantry Division headquarters in Preny, France, on November 11, the commander, Maj. Gen. LeRoy Irwin explains the layout of the Verdun fortified group to the visiting US Army chief of staff, Gen. George Marshall. To Irwin's left is the XX Corps commander, Maj. Gen. Walton Walker and Lt. Gen. George Patton. (NARA)

One element of the XIX TAC air preparations for Operation *Madison* was a series of decapitation strikes against key German headquarters that had been identified by Allied intelligence. On November 8, P-47 Thunderbolts of the 405th Fighter Group dive-bombed this headquarters of the 17. SS-Panzergrenadier-Division in Peltre where the divisional intelligence and operations staff was located, killing or wounding many of the headquarters officers. (NARA)

Antwerp was cleared. This was the principal mission of Montgomery's British/Canadian 21st Army Group. Once Antwerp was open, Eisenhower anticipated a three-phase campaign starting with the destruction of German forces on the western side of the Rhine, the Rhine crossing and, finally, the advance into Germany. The focus of the campaign would be in the north, primarily Montgomery's 21st Army Group, and the two northern field armies of Bradley's 12th Army Group – Ninth US Army and First US Army. Patton's Third US Army, although part of Bradley's command, was geographically separated from the other field armies by the Ardennes region, which Bradley felt was unsuitable for operation and which was screened by a modest force only a corps in size. Patton's force abutted the Seventh US Army to the south in Alsace, part of Lt. Gen. Jacob Dever's 6th Army Group.

By late October, Eisenhower began discussions with the field army commanders about the conduct of the forthcoming operations, which were expected to resume in early November. Patton's tactical objective was to overcome the Metz defenses with the hope that if they could be overwhelmed quickly enough then the Siegfried Line would be weakly held and subject to widespread penetration. The ultimate operational objective was to destroy as much of AOK 1 as possible and to reach the Rhine near Mainz and Mannheim.

The plan for the November attack was codenamed Operation *Madison*. At the time, Patton's forces had been trimmed back to only two operational corps after XV Corps had been transferred to the neighboring Seventh US

Army in Alsace. This consisted of Walker's XX Corps facing Metz, and Eddy's XII Corps on the Seille River. A third corps headquarters, Milliken's III Corps, arrived in November but did not have divisions yet assigned and so did not participate in the attack. The focus of fighting in September 1944 had been in Eddy's XII Corps sector; during the November fighting, the focus was on Walker's XX Corps since they faced the formidable barrier of the Metz defensive belt.

The plans by Walker's XX Corps had been modified by the sobering experience of the Fort Driant battle that took place during the October lull. This battle is described in more detail below. Early XX Corps plans for the offensive spoke of the encirclement and reduction of the Metz fortifications as the principal mission. The final field orders moved away from the mission of reducing the forts, and instead aimed at the "destruction or capture of the Metz garrison, without the investiture or siege of the Metz forts."

Since the front had been static for most of October and the first week of November, the XX Corps plan included a significant deception effort to prevent the Germans from identifying the focus of the main attacks. A fake radio network was created to mimic the 14th Armored Division which was not yet in theater, placing it to the northwest of Thionville. Immediately prior to the execution of Operation *Madison*, the 95th Infantry Division and 10th Armored Division were shifted to the Thionville axis under a blanket of radio silence. The role of the 95th Division was to stage a "demonstration" with a battalion-sized force at the outset of the operation to confuse the Germans regarding the main axis of attack. The main attack would by a pincer movement consisting of the 90th Division from the Thionville area north of Metz, and the 5th Infantry Division from the Arnaville bridgehead to the south of Metz. The 10th Armored Division was intended as the exploitation force which would follow the 90th Division attack, and then race to the Saar River. The 95th Division's role would be to seize Metz from the west which would allow the remainder of the corps to continue its mission of seizing a bridgehead around Sarreburg following the disruption and destruction of the AOK 1 forces in the Metz pocket.

One of the more curious preparatory actions for the offensive was an air attack on the Etang-de-Lindre dam near Dieuze. This large artificial lake had been regarded as a military asset for centuries since the Seille area nearby could be inundated by opening the dam's floodgates. This had been done in the 1870 Franco-Prussian War, and the US Army decided to preempt the German use of the dam by draining it before the attack. After XII Corps engineers built a flood control system to channel the spill, the dam was attacked on October 20 by two P-47 squadrons from the 362nd Fighter Group using 1,000lb bombs which made a 15-yard breach in it.

GERMAN PLANS

By the mid-autumn of 1944, Hitler and the OKW (Oberkommando der Wehrmacht: Armed Forces High Command) had a sound appreciation of Allied operational plans, particularly the focus on Antwerp and approach to the Ruhr via the Aachen–Stolberg corridor. Since preparations for the Ardennes offensive were well under way by early November, the OKW was faced with the difficult task of keeping the best units, especially the Panzer divisions, in reserve in the Eifel while trying to restrain the Allied advances with a bare minimum of forces. As in the Allied case, the field armies in the northern sector on the Scheldt and around Aachen received priority. As part of this process, Heeresgruppe G was substantially weakened in mid-October, by withdrawing 5. Panzerarmee to the Aachen sector in anticipation of its eventual use in the Ardennes offensive. On top of this, both the 3. and 15. Panzergrenadier-Divisionen were withdrawn into OKW reserve.

In view of its weakened state, Heeresgruppe G recommended that Metz be abandoned and that the main defense line be erected along the Westwall on the Saar River; Hitler rejected any idea of giving up Metz without a fight and declared it a fortress (*Festung*) that would fight to the last man. By early November, it was clear that Patton's Third US Army had deployed two strong groupings on either side of Metz and so an attack was anticipated. Hitler insisted that a deep artillery barrier be prepared to shield the Saar region, and the emphasis on the allocation of reinforcements was on *Festung-Artillerie* units. Hitler hoped that the extensive fortification work on the West-Stellung as well as the Metz fortress belt would be an adequate barrier against an American attack in Lorraine in November.

The task facing Gen. Balck and Heeresgruppe G was to defend Lorraine with substantially inferior forces. The chart below shows the Heeresgruppe G assessment of the correlation of forces in the focal point sector (*Schwerpunkt*) of XIII SS-AK in November 1944; in other sectors the correlation was even worse.

Heeresgruppe G assessment of correlation of forces in Lorraine

	US	German
Tanks	570	60
Troops	24,000	5,318
Light field guns	318	113
Heavy field guns	60	64
Daily artillery expenditure (rounds)	10,000	5,200
Mortars	580	208
Machine guns	4,270	1,570

Heeresgruppe G was warned that they should not expect much in the way of Luftwaffe support, either in the form of reconnaissance or fighter cover; fighter bomber and bomber support was out of the question. Aside from 11. Panzer-Division, there was no substantial reserve available to AOK 1 in the Metz sector. Owing to the extremely uneven balance of forces, Balck hoped to rely on those assets where the Germans were closer to parity, especially artillery. In addition, there was some hope that the extensive work on field fortifications and the West-Stellung could help stymie an American advance. German officers were comforted by the rule-of-thumb that it takes a three-to-one advantage to overcome a strongly defended position, and some officers argued that a heavily fortified defense like Metz required a six-to-one advantage. One of the few consolations in the picture was the lull in the fighting through most of October which allowed AOK 1 to rebuild its battered divisions and to conduct further field fortification work.

Balck's tactical approach was to employ elastic defense tactics first developed in 1917–18 and subsequently applied on the Russian front in 1943–44. Extensive defense positions located near the main line of resistance (MLR) would be identified by enemy intelligence and pre-registered prior to an offensive by the enemy artillery. As a result, a modest screening force was left forward, and the main defense force kept about 1.2–2 miles (2–3km) behind the forward line to prevent destruction by the enemy preparatory barrages. The MLR was reinforced with successive, prepared fortified lines to permit orderly withdrawal, and oblique defense lines (Riegel-Stellungen) were added to the defenses to prevent defensive lines being overwhelmed from the flank in the event of a penetration at one point on the front. Although Balck and Knobelsdorff intended to use elastic defense tactics, Hitler's admonition that Metz must be held to the last created a tactical paradox. Their solution to this dilemma was to defend Metz with a plausible, though hardly imposing force based mainly around the 462. Volksgrenadier-Division. As will be seen later, this division was regarded as expendable, and when AOK 1 was threatened with envelopment by the American pincer attack, the division was abandoned to its fate in Metz along with the assorted fortress garrisons while AOK 1 withdrew to successive West-Stellung defense lines.

The original OKW plan called for the AOK 1 forces in the Metz–Diedenhofen fortified zone to allow themselves to be surrounded and then to tie down US forces through protracted resistance. General Knobelsdorff strongly opposed this approach, arguing that the forces available to AOK 1 were so immobile and weak that the US Army would simply bypass the surrounded forces and move on to the east. OKW acknowledged this viewpoint in October and changed the plans accordingly which implied that the flanks had to be more securely defended, notably the river crossing areas on either side of Diedenhofen (Thionville) and the area around the Arnaville bridgehead.

The AOK 1 assessment of US intentions was basically correct, and assumed a push on Metz from either side followed by a push to Saarbrücken. However, AOK 1 assumed that the main thrust would come from XII Corps northeast of Nancy towards Metz, and underestimated the threat posed by XX Corps from Thionville. As a result, AOK 1 assessed the XIII SS-AK sector as being the focal point (*Schwehrpunkt*) and especially the Delme Ridge, a traditional defensive position blocking the "Lorraine Gateway." Field fortification efforts concentrated on the Delme Ridge and surrounding areas with AOK 1 personnel responsible for the forward defenses while the Wehrkreis XII fortification engineers dealt with deep defenses further east. In addition, the reserves available to AOK 1, notably the 11. Panzer-Division, were located mainly to the northeast of the Delme Ridge. The threat from the Thionville sector was judged less ominous since the Moselle River bifurcated this sector, creating a natural tank barrier that would slow the exploitation of armor towards Saarbrücken. The only army reserve in this sector was a regiment from the overextended 19. Volksgrenadier-Division. Anti-tank guns were in such short supply that the emphasis on anti-tank defense turned to extensive minefields which were planted in October 1944; a special anti-tank gun battalion was rushed to the sector after the start of the American attacks.

Heeresgruppe G had dispatched about ten battalions including *Festung-MG* and *Ersatz-Ausbildungs* (replacement and training) units to AOK 1 in October in hopes of adding to the depth of the defenses. However, AOK 1 was so thin on troops that many of these units were broken up into companies which were then doled out to the divisions as fillers to make up for combat losses in September. Artillery ammunition was in short supply, and as a result, no preparatory bombardment of American assembly areas was possible in early November when the US attack seemed imminent.

West-Stellung defense lines in Lorraine

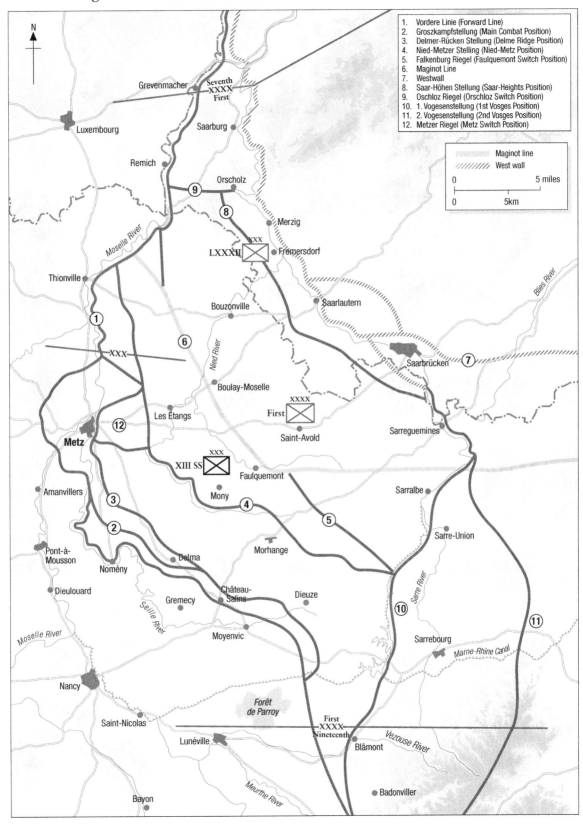

Legend:
1. Vordere Linie (Forward Line)
2. Groszkampfstellung (Main Combat Position)
3. Delmer-Rücken Stellung (Delme Ridge Position)
4. Nied-Metzer Stelling (Nied-Metz Position)
5. Falkenburg Riegel (Faulquemont Switch Position)
6. Maginot Line
7. Westwall
8. Saar-Höhen Stellung (Saar-Heights Position)
9. Oschloz Riegel (Orschloz Switch Position)
10. 1. Vogesenstellung (1st Vosges Position)
11. 2. Vogesenstellung (2nd Vosges Position)
12. Metzer Riegel (Metz Switch Position)

CAMPAIGN

OPERATION *THUNDERBOLT*: FORT DRIANT

Fort Driant had been a thorn in the side of XX Corps during the Moselle River crossing attempts in early September, and it was presumed that the fort would have to be taken or neutralized as a preliminary step to the eventual reduction of Metz. The old fort had not been occupied by German troops earlier in 1944 and its casernes and underground tunnels had been used as aircraft assembly shops for the VDM plant (Vereinigten Deustchen Metallwerke) after the original Frankfurt factory had been bombed.

On August 27, General der Infanterie Walter Schroth, commander of Wehrkreis XII, ordered Fahnenjunkerschule VI Metz (the Metz officer candidate's school) to form an improvised battlegroup to help defend the city. It was first called Kampfgruppe von Siegroth and later Kampfgruppe Stössel after a change in school commanders. The school was organized into three *Lehrgänge* (training battalions) each with four *Inspektionen* (training companies) – three infantry and one heavy weapons company. The regiment numbered about 1,500 troops. These were mostly combat-hardened NCOs who had received field promotions on the Eastern Front, and who were completing their formal training. The first actions of the group in early September were to organize straggler collection points around the city to cull retreating columns for troops and equipment; some 4,000 troops and 400 vehicles were collected in the process which were amalgamated into various replacement battalions. Kampfgruppe Stössel was deployed along a 12-mile (20km) frontage from Armanvillers through Gravelotte to Ars-sur-Moselle to defend against the approaching American XX Corps. These battalions constructed fieldworks along the Moselle River until first contact with US troops in early September. The Ars-sur-Moselle sector was assigned to Lehrgang 3, commanded by one of the school instructors, 30-year-old Hauptmann August Weiler, a decorated combat veteran with two Iron Crosses. At first, the MLR was established behind Feste Kronprinz (Fort Driant) since the senior commanders felt that the old forts had no defensive value. A single platoon was placed near Fort Driant as an outpost in front of the main line.

The commander of the battalion's heavy weapons company, Hauptmann Hinkmann, found that there was ample ammunition in the fort even if most of the guns were not immediately functional. Hinkmann began steps to rejuvenate the two 100mm Krupp howitzers in the Moselbatterie which

Festung Metz

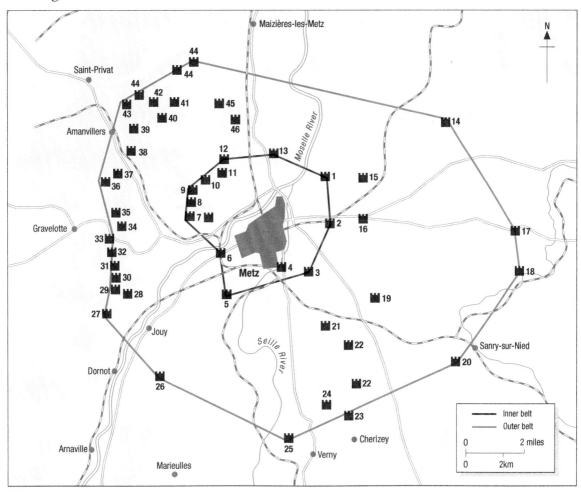

	French name	German name		French name	German name
Inner Belt			**23**	Groupe fortifié l'Yser	Feste Luitpold
1	Fort Saint-Julien	Feste Manteuffel	**24**	Batterie du Bois des Veaux	Schirmlafettenbatterie Hospitalwald
2	Fort des Bottes	Feste Zastrow	**25**	Groupe fortifié l'Aisne	Feste Wagner
3	Fort de Queuleu	Feste Goeben	**26**	Groupe fortifié Verdun	Feste Graf von Haeseler
4	Batterie cuirassée du Sablon	Panzerbatterie Sablon	**27**	Groupe fortifié Driant	Feste Kronprinz
5	Fort Saint-Privat	Feste Württemberg	**28**	Batterie d'Ars	Schirmlafettenbatterie Ars an der Mosel
6	Batterie de Canal	Kanalbatterie	**28**	Fort de Marival	Zwischenwerke Marival
7	Groupe fortifié Saint-Quentin	Panzerbatterie Friedrich-Karl	**30**	Ouvrage de Vaux	Zwischenwerke Vaux
8	Batteries cuirassées Plappeville	Panzerbatterien Plappeville	**31**	Ouvrage de Bois-le-Dame	Zwischenwerke Bois-la-Dame
9	Fort de Plappeville	Feste von Alvensleben	**32**	Ouvrage de Jussy	Zwischenwerke Jussy
10	Fort Decaen	Feste Schwerin	**33**	Ouvrage de Saint-Hubert	Zwischenwerke St. Hubert
11	Batteries cuirassées du Chene	Panzerbatterien Westeiche und Osteiche	**34**	Groupe fortifié Jeanne d'Arc	Feste Kaiserin
12	Fort Deroulede	Feste Kameke	**35**	Caserne forte de Moscou	Infanterieraum 6
13	Fort Gambetta	Feste Hindersin	**36**	Groupe fortifié Francois de Guise	Feste Leipzig
			37	Batterie Montvaux	Schirmlafettenbatterie Montvaux
Outer belt			**38**	Caserne fort de Saint-Vincent	Infanterieraum 3-St. Vincent
14	Ouvrage Sainte-Barbe	Vorgeschobene Batterie St. Barbe	**39**	Ouvrage Kellerman	Wolfsberg-Stellung
15	Fort Champagne	Infanteriewerk Mey	**40**	Groupe fortifié Lorraine	Feste Lothringen
16	Fort de Lauvalliere	Infanteriewerk Bellecroix	**41**	Ouvrage Richepanse	Vemont-Stellung
17	Ouvrage de Silly	Vorgeschobene Batterie Silly	**42**	Redoubte Lasalle	-
18	Ouvrage de Mont	Vorgeschobene Batterie Mont	**43**	Ouvrages des Carrières d'Amanvillers	Steinbruch-Stellung
19	La Marne	Feste von der Goltz	**44**	Ouvrage Canrobert	Horimont-Befestigungen
20	Ouvrage de Sorbey	Vorgeschobene Batterie Sorbey	**45**	Ouvrage du Bois de la Julière	Infanterieraum 1 St. Anne
21	Batterie de Crépy	Schirmlafettenbatterie Crépy	**46**	Batterie de Sainte-Agathe	Schirmlafettenbatterie St. Agathe
22	Ouvrage de Chesny	Schirmlafettenbatterie Chesny			

AIR STRIKE ON FORT DRIANT (pp. 36–37)

The XIX Tactical Air Command (XIX TAC) supporting Patton's Third US Army relied on P-47 fighter-bombers for most of its air support effort in the autumn of 1944. The initial attempts to knock out Fort Driant **(1)** in the third week of September 1944 employed dive-bombing attacks against the artillery casemates and casernes. Although these attacks were reasonably accurate, the bombs available to the P-47 squadrons, mainly the standard 500lb high-explosive bomb, was not effective in demolishing the thick earth and concrete protecting the forts. Attempts were also made to attack the forts in the area using B-26 Marauder bombers using larger 1,000 and 2,000lb semi-armor-piercing (SAP) bombs. The only weapon that was consistently effective against the concrete structures was the 2,000lb bomb and this did not become evident until after some of the forts were captured. In the meantime, the P-47 squadrons were suspicious of the effectiveness of their 500lb bombs and began to switch to the use of napalm as a more efficient method to attack the forts. It first used napalm in the air strikes on September 21.

One of the most active units in the air campaign in Lorraine was the 405th Fighter Group, equipped with P-47D fighter-bombers. The 405th Fighter Group had already participated in the Normandy campaign as part of IX TAC, and was assigned to support Patton's Third Army under XIX TAC on August 5, 1944. During mid-September, the group was heavily involved in supporting the 4th Armored Division in the XII Corps sector during the tank battles around Arracourt. In late September, the group began to support the XX Corps efforts along the Moselle, including air attacks on Fort Driant as seen here. The three squadrons of the group were distinguished by different colors on the nose and tail, with the 509th Fighter Squadron **(2)** using red as seen here.

Officers of the 2nd Battalion, 11th Infantry, hold a meeting on October 6 in the woods below Fort Driant prior to the next attack. The figure to the far left is Capt. Jack Gerrie, Co. G commander, and next to him is Major John Russell, the battalion commander. (NARA)

overlooked the Moselle crossing site of the 11th Infantry, 5th Division, near Dornot. Hinkmann's crews began firing on the Dornot bridgehead on September 10, and the following day, XX Corps artillery targeted the site, hitting one of the armored cupolas and killing three crewmen. However, the gun was functional again within a half-hour, ample testament to the battery's armor. By September 15, Hinkmann's company had most of the guns in the main fort operational and they took part in the final attempts to smash another 5th Division bridgehead near Arnaville.

Hinkmann's success in bringing the gun batteries back to life prompted the Festung Metz command to rejuvenate the fort itself. Soldiers were dispatched to the fort and began creating fieldworks at weak points, especially on the northwestern corner. The original Feste Kronprinz had been designed to accommodate a garrison of 1,800 troops in five fortified casernes and was armed with five batteries – a total of eight 100mm and six 150mm howitzers in armored cupolas. It covered an area of about 85 acres (35 hectares). By mid-September, the fort was held by troops of 10./Kampfgruppe Stössel supplemented by some troops of Hinkmann's heavy-weapons' company and about 45 artillery troops from HKAA 938 (Heeres-Küsten-Artillerie-Abteilung) a former Atlantic Wall coastal artillery regiment. In late September, the Festung Metz commanders created a new Festungsgruppe Driant based on Weiler's Lehrgang 3, including three infantry companies (5., 9. and 10./Kampgruppe Stössel) which increased the strength of the fort's garrison from about 100 to 400–500 troops by the end of September.

Walker's XX Corps attempted to secure several Moselle River crossings on the run starting on September 7. The hasty 11th Infantry crossing attempt at Dornot was pushed back over the river, in part due to the constant artillery fire from Fort Driant and the neighboring Fort Jeanne d'Arc (Feste Kaiserin). The 2/11th Regiment was redeployed from the failed Dornot bridgehead to contain Fort Driant. The battalion had suffered nearly 50 percent casualties during the bridgehead attempt, and spent the next few weeks absorbing replacements.

A German prisoner captured near Fort Driant on September 20 indicated that the fort was being held by only 100–120 men, which led to the widespread American belief that the fort was not well defended. One of the American company commanders involved in the first attacks indicated that "Fort Driant is manned by about 100 old men and boys, whose morale is low. They will probably not make a determined effort to hold the fort." At the time, the 11th Regiment had no detailed plans of the fort beyond small-scale maps and aerial photos that made the fort look largely deserted and failed to reveal the extensive fields of barb wire.

The serious underestimation of the defenses at the fort led the 11th Infantry's commander, Colonel Charles Yuill, to propose to the 5th Division headquarters that the 2/11th Infantry would be sufficient to seize the fort and that it would be a good morale booster for the battalion after its heavy losses at Dornot while at the same time being a useful method of providing battle indoctrination to the many green replacements which made up half the battalion's strength. Major-General LeRoy Irwin, the 5th Division commander, approved the plan and the 2/11th Infantry began training to assault the fort on September 21.

On September 17, Walker's XX Corps staff had outlined a plan to begin a more systematic reduction of Metz codenamed Operation *Thunderbolt*. The first phase of *Thunderbolt* included an assault on Fort Driant, though at this stage it had no direct connection to the actions being taken by the 5th Infantry Division. Operation *Thunderbolt* proved short lived when Eisenhower's September 22 instructions imposed a temporary moratorium

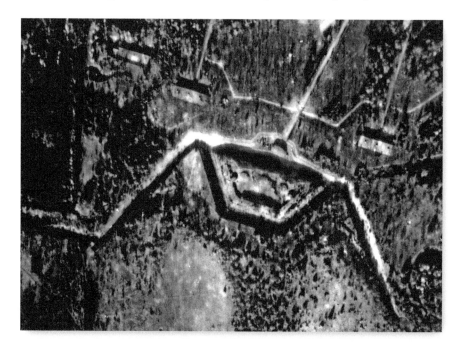

This is an overhead reconnaissance photo of Fort Driant taken on September 28. It shows the main fort while behind it are three of the gun casemates, L, M, and O from right to left. Most of the fighting took part in the southwest corner of the fort which was over to the right of this photo and largely out of view. (MHI)

on major operations. Eisenhower's orders did not exclude small-unit action: battalion-size or smaller. As a result, Yuill's plan to seize Fort Driant proceeded independently of the abandoned Operation *Thunderbolt*. Yuill's overconfidence, Eisenhower's moratorium and the overextension of the 5th Division lines all contributed to the decision to attack the fort with only a single battalion. There was also the unfounded presumption that modern airpower and artillery would make short work of the fort's antiquated defenses. Eleven P-47 fighter-bombers conducted bombing runs on the fort on September 24 followed by a heavier attack by 35 aircraft on September 26. The 2/11th Infantry sent a large patrol near the fort after the September 26 bombing, but it was prevented from reaching it by heavy machine-gun and mortar fire. The attack was finally scheduled for September 27 and the assault force consisted of the 2/11th Infantry with tank, artillery, and engineer support. Since the 2/11th Infantry had suffered such heavy casualties at Dornot, Co. B from 1/11th Infantry was substituted for Co. F, 2/11th Infantry, which was still too battered to participate.

At 0930hrs September 27, 12 P-47 Thunderbolts of the 405th Fighter Group bombed the fort, followed by another squadron with napalm and machine-gun strafing later in the morning. During the late morning and early afternoon, artillery bombarded the fort. The 2/11th Infantry began the attack at 1400 hours led by Company E against the northwest perimeter of the fort. The infantry were able to penetrate into the outer barb-wire field in front of the fort, but were soon forced to ground by machine-gun fire, and later by mortars and artillery. Attempts to use pole charges against the machine-gun pillboxes were frustrated by the extensive fields of barb wire shielding the fort. It was soon evident that the attack had been much too small and the company withdrew under the cover of darkness to the line of departure where they dug in. American casualties had been light, about 18 men.

The 11th Infantry planned to resume the attack the following day, but in the meantime, had obtained a set of plans of the fort from French officers.

An aerial view of Fort Driant taken by an artillery spotter plane of the 5th Infantry Division on September 29. The town of Ars-sur-Moselle can be seen behind the fort to the southeast. The initial attack on the fort took place in the northwest corner on the left side of this photo while the subsequent October fighting took place on the opposite side to right of the main fort complex. (NARA)

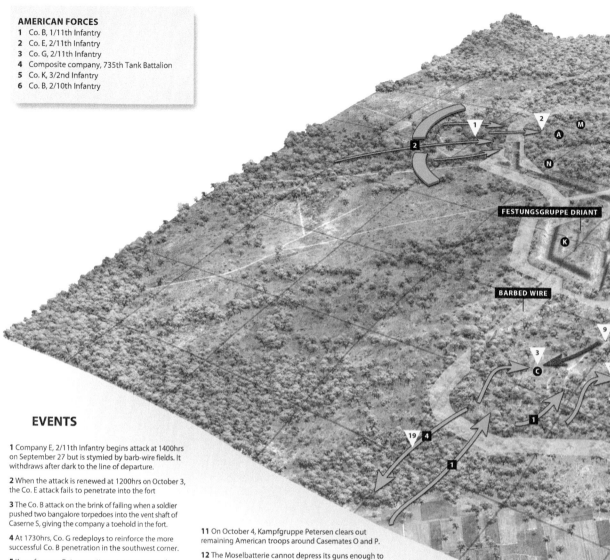

AMERICAN FORCES

1 Co. B, 1/11th Infantry
2 Co. E, 2/11th Infantry
3 Co. G, 2/11th Infantry
4 Composite company, 735th Tank Battalion
5 Co. K, 3/2nd Infantry
6 Co. B, 2/10th Infantry

FESTUNGSGRUPPE DRIANT

BARBED WIRE

YUILL

EVENTS

1 Company E, 2/11th Infantry begins attack at 1400hrs on September 27 but is stymied by barb-wire fields. It withdraws after dark to the line of departure.

2 When the attack is renewed at 1200hrs on October 3, the Co. E attack fails to penetrate into the fort

3 The Co. B attack on the brink of failing when a soldier pushed two bangalore torpedoes into the vent shaft of Caserne S, giving the company a toehold in the fort.

4 At 1730hrs, Co. G redeploys to reinforce the more successful Co. B penetration in the southwest corner.

5 Kampfgruppe Petersen attempts to stage a major counterattack against Co. E around 1800hrs, but was bombed by orbiting P-47 fighters.

6 The sudden infusion of Co. G troops leads to a penetration into the fort as far as Casemates O and P by 1830hrs.

7 G/11th Infantry tries to push into the center of the fort, but around 1900hrs the German garrison stages a major counterattack which forces the American company into retreat.

8 Late on October 2, Co. G rallies along a defense line southeast of Battery G.

9 Festungsgruppe Driant retires into bunkers and underground shelters and counters US attack by calling in artillery fire from nearby Fort Verdun and Fort Marival. Kampfgruppe Petersen attacks Casernes R and S, but suffers heavy losses.

10 3./Ausbildungs-Battalion 208 with about 150 troops attempts to reinforce Festungsgruppe Driant after dark on October 3-4, but is stymied by American artillery; the battalion gradually makes its way into the fort the next day.

11 On October 4, Kampfgruppe Petersen clears out remaining American troops around Casemates O and P.

12 The Moselbatterie cannot depress its guns enough to hit nearby US positions, so on October 4, the guns are used to interdict American reinforcements coming up the hill on the southwest corner of the fort by firing into the trees which causes overhead airbursts.

13 On October 4–5, reinforcements from Co. K, 2nd Infantry, try to push into southeast corner of fort near Caserne Y but are halted by German counterattacks.

14 A pair of Jagdpanzer IV tank destroyers enters the fort around 0715hrs on October 6 to support an attack by Fusilier-Kompanie 19. The attack around 0830hrs withers under American fire, but the tank destroyers knock out two American tanks.

On the evening of October 6, the decimated US units in the southwest corner of the fort are replaced by companies from the 10th Infantry with plans to resume the attack on October 7.

15 The US attacks resume on October 7, with Co. B, 2nd Infantry, again trying to clear the south-east corner of the fort, but a German counterattack overran two platoons from B/2nd Infantry including the company commander.

16 On October 7, about 160 troops of 3./, and 4./Kampfgruppe Stössel redeploy out of fort to the northwest in hopes of attacking US troops in front of the fort, but the attack fails to materialize due to artillery.

17 The 3/2nd Infantry relieves 2/2nd Infantry in attempts to secure the underground passageway between Caserne R and Casemate P but are frustrated by armored doors and debris.

18 German counter-mining teams detonate explosives in underground passageway around 1650hrs, October 9, ending this attempt to break into the gun casemates.

19 The last US troops withdrew from Fort Driant at 2330hrs, October 12 and detonations inside the fort continued into the early morning hours of October 13.

ATTACK ON FORT DRIANT, SEPTEMBER 27–OCTOBER 12, 1944

The US 11th Infantry gets bogged down in the face of strong German defenses

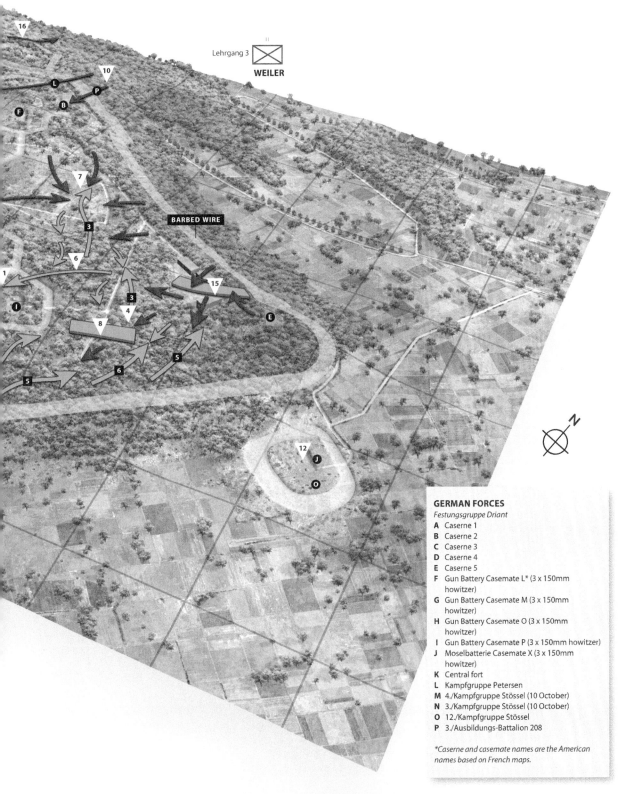

Note: Gridlines are shown at intervals of 200m/218yds

Lehrgang 3 ⊠
WEILER

BARBED WIRE

GERMAN FORCES
Festungsgruppe Driant
A Caserne 1
B Caserne 2
C Caserne 3
D Caserne 4
E Caserne 5
F Gun Battery Casemate L* (3 x 150mm howitzer)
G Gun Battery Casemate M (3 x 150mm howitzer)
H Gun Battery Casemate O (3 x 150mm howitzer)
I Gun Battery Casemate P (3 x 150mm howitzer)
J Moselbatterie Casemate X (3 x 150mm howitzer)
K Central fort
L Kampfgruppe Petersen
M 4./Kampfgruppe Stössel (10 October)
N 3./Kampfgruppe Stössel (10 October)
O 12./Kampfgruppe Stössel
P 3./Ausbildungs-Battalion 208

Caserne and casemate names are the American names based on French maps.

43

These confirmed that the defense of the fort had been substantially underestimated. Even Patton, well versed in the military history of the region, mistakenly referred to the forts as "Vauban-era" when in fact they were substantially more modern and comparable with French forts like Fort Douamont at Verdun that had been the scene of such infernal fighting in World War I.

The initial attack also convinced the Festung Metz command to further reinforce the fort's defenses. The 4./Kampfgruppe Stössel was taken off the Moselle front to the Seekt Kaserne at Verny where it was reconfigured as a heavy-weapons company with additional machine guns and flame-throwers. It was redesignated as Kampfgruppe Petersen and arrived at the fort on October 2. Additional reinforcements were sent to the fort including about 120 replacement troops of 3./Ausbildungs-Battalion 208 which also reached

the outskirts of the fort on October 2, bringing the fort's strength to about five infantry companies plus various supporting troops.

On September 28, the 5th Division commander, Maj. Gen. LeRoy Irwin met with Patton and Walker to discuss the general progress of the campaign in the Metz sector. Irwin recommended that Fort Driant be bypassed and surrounded, but the Division was spread so thinly over such a wide front that sufficient troops were simply not available for such an effort. At the time, the 5th Infantry Division was holding a front 12 miles (20km) wide, bifurcated by the Moselle, and had suffered 3,056 casualties in September. Walker insinuated that the first attack had failed because of a lack of aggressive personal leadership by the regimental and battalion commanders. A new attack plan was drawn up, bolstered by more thorough knowledge of the fort and more comprehensive preparations and Patton approved it on September 29. Division engineers began manufacturing a variety of infantry assault devices including satchel charges, pole charges to attack the pillboxes, and Bangalore torpedoes to breach the barb wire. Since the infantry-borne Bangalore torpedoes were too short to breach the deep wire obstacles, the 735th Tank Battalion began to construct "snakes" – lengths of pipe filled with explosive that could be pushed by the tanks under the wire and then remotely detonated. The tank support was reinforced to create a composite company consisting of 11 M4A3(76mm) medium tanks, five M5A1 light tanks, four M4 (105mm) assault guns and two M4 tank dozers for filling the dry moats. A section of M12 155mm self-propelled guns from the 558th Field Artillery Battalion was stationed near the fort to conduct direct fire against the artillery cupolas. There were also plans to attack the fort with additional air strikes by medium bombers using heavier bombs that offered better performance against concrete, as well as fighter-bombers using napalm.

A total of 23 field artillery battalions conducted a preliminary artillery bombardment on October 2, one of the most concentrated artillery attacks so far in Europe in 1944 against such a small target. Although not evident at

During the fighting at Fort Driant, a section of two M12 155mm GMCs of the 558th Field Artillery Battalion under the command of Lt. Ralph Major were moved into the woods adjacent to the fort and began a systematic campaign to knock out the gun cupolas with direct fire from a range of 800 yards (730m). Although the 155mm gun could not penetrate the 300mm-thick armor of the cupolas, the force of the impact was often enough to disable the turret, and the section was credited with putting at least two cupolas out of action. (NARA)

BLASTING THE MOSELLE BRIDGEHEAD (pp. 46–47)

Lacking any significant air support, the most powerful long-range weapons available to AOK 1 were a half-dozen railway guns subordinated to the Eisenbahn-Artillerie-Abteilung 640 Stab. Four of these were the 28cm K5 (E), which had an effective range of 38 miles (62km) when firing the 255kg (565lb) Gr 35 projectile. These were nicknamed "Schlanke Bertha" (Slender Bertha) by their German crews, but better known as "Anzio Annie" by the US Army who encountered this type of weapon at the Anzio beachhead. The Eisenbahn-Artillerie-Abteilung 640 staff had served on the Russian Front during the siege of Leningrad in 1942, and were subsequently transferred to southern France where they controlled railway artillery batteries there until Operation *Dragoon* in August 1944. During the retreat up the Rhône Valley most of its railway guns were lost in the Montelimar pocket, and those in service in Lorraine came mainly from batteries that had served on the Atlantikwall.

This particular K5 (E) **(1)** gun was deployed at Ébersviller in the railway tunnel on the Metz–Bouzonville line. The gun lacked the usual turntable for aiming, and the Ébersviller site was chosen since there was a tunnel to shield the gun from Allied air attack, and the track on the western side of the tunnel was curved,

providing a wide range of aiming angles towards Thionville. The westbound tunnel **(2)** was used to house four locomotives, ammunition cars, and associated rolling stock including a kitchen car for the gun crew. The gun would be pushed out to pre-surveyed points along the track for firing, and then pulled back into the tunnel.

It entered combat use from this site in late September and early October, firing at XX Corps targets including the corps headquarters on October 5 and 7. This elicited the attention of the XX Corps artillery staff which discovered its location and began counter-battery fire on Sunday October 8 using an 8in. gun and a 240mm "Black Dragon" howitzer. The K5(E) was severely damaged during this exchange and pulled back for repair. A K5(E) was again deployed in this sector in November 1944, firing on Jarny-Conflans on November 13–14, but from records it is unclear whether it was a different gun or the original one that had been repaired. Another K5(E) gun, dubbed the "Nancy Gun" by US troops, was active in the XII Corps sector and one round struck near the Corps Command Post in Nancy on October 24. It was subsequently put out of action by air attacks.

the time, the artillery bombardment was almost completely ineffective as the fort had been designed to absorb far heavier bombardment by large-caliber siege artillery. The infantry attack was supposed to jump off at 0910hrs on October 3, but it was continually delayed by an anticipated medium-bomber attack that failed to materialize owing to poor weather. Losing patience, the 11th Infantry HQ ordered the attack to start at noon. Company E, supported by Co. G, attacked the same section of the fort in the northwest as the first attack, while Co. B attacked the southwest corner.

Once again, the Co. E attack on the northwest corner was stopped cold without significant penetration. Once the American infantry began moving towards the fort, the assembly areas were subjected to a severe pounding from neighboring German forts in the prescribed fashion. The "snake" tanks were not effective in breaching the wire obstructions because of the difficulty in moving them over rough terrain; the few snakes that reached the outer edge of the fort were ineffective owing to the high walls surrounding the dry moats and neither dozer tank reached the area in time to assist in the breaching. Company B managed to make its way through the defenses in the southwest corner with the tanks helping to breach the barb-wire fields. The fortified casernes in this sector had walls 5ft (1.5m) thick and these proved impervious to the direct fire of the M4(105mm) assault guns. It seemed that the attack might fail, but Pvt. Robert Holmlund spotted a ventilator shaft on top of a caserne, and pushed two Bangalore torpedoes into it. The ensuing blast forced the German defenders out of a portion of the caserne, which was soon occupied by an American infantry squad.

Around 1730hrs, Co. G shifted from the northwest sector to reinforce the more successful Co. B penetration in the southwest corner. While this was taking place, the Festung Driant garrison attempted to stage a major counterattack, which was smashed by orbiting P-47 fighters with 22 500lb bombs. German attempts to reinforce the fort via the wooded trails to the east were repeatedly halted by artillery, delaying the arrival of two more companies of infantry on October 3. The sudden infusion of the Co. G troops and the decimation of the German counterattack force led to a sudden penetration into the fort in the late evening, but it was to little avail as the troops could not break into the fortified casernes or gun casemate buildings aside from the two casernes captured in the initial attacks. After dark, the garrison staged another counterattack, which forced Co. G to withdraw and badly disrupted Co. B. Reinforcements from Co. K, 2nd Infantry, arrived in the nick of time to prevent a rout.

The second day of fighting proved to be a costly stalemate. The German garrison used the forts as intended, and artillery fire from nearby forts combined with heavy machine-gun fire swept the exterior of Fort Driant clean of attacking infantry. The guns in the fort itself could not be depressed sufficiently to be used in direct fire, but the Moselbatterie was able to fire against the woods near the approach route of the American forces on the southwest corner of the fort causing airburst high in the trees, making reinforcement more difficult. The surface of the fort was so hazardous that the American infantry attempted to conduct their attacks through the underground tunnels, most of which were blocked by armored doors. In the first 24 hours of the attack, the US forces assaulting the southwestern sector suffered 50 percent casualties. Tanks were one of the few means for the American attackers to retain some measure of control above ground, and so they were vigorously assaulted by special German anti-tank teams using

Panzerfaust and Puppchen anti-tank rocket launchers. On the first day of fighting, five tanks were knocked out; by October 4 nine of the 12 American tanks inside the fort were out of operation, five by enemy action. Major Ferris Church, commander of the 2/11th Infantry grimly reported:

> The situation is critical. A couple more barrages and another counterattack and we are sunk. We have no men, our equipment is shot and we just can't go on. The troops in G Company are done, they are just there what's left of them. Enemy has infiltrated and pinned what is here down. We cannot advance nor can K Co. B Co. is in the same shape I'm in. We cannot delay any longer on replacement. We may be able to hold out till dark but if anything happens this afternoon, I can make no predictions. The enemy artillery is butchering these troops until we have nothing left to hold with. We cannot get out to get out wounded and there is a hell of a lot of dead and missing. There is only one answer the way things stand. First either to withdraw and saturate it with heavy bombers or reinforce with a hell of a strong force. This strong force might hold here but eventually they'll get it by artillery fire. They have all this zeroed in by artillery.

With the situation turning desperate, and under pressure from Maj. Gen. Walker to complete the assignment, on October 5, Maj. Gen. Irwin decided to reinforce rather than abandon the attack. Brig. Gen. A. D. Warnock, the assistant division commander, was placed in charge, and Irwin began to scour his overextended division for reinforcements. On the evening of October 6, the decimated units in the southwest corner of the fort were replaced by companies from the 10th Infantry with plans to resume the attack on October 7.

The German garrison continued to receive reinforcements along the wooded roads from Ars-sur-Moselle, in spite of the best efforts of the US artillery to keep the fort sealed off. Kampfgruppe Petersen was the main counterattack force, and newly arrived infantry companies were repeatedly added to it to conduct successive counterattacks. On the evening of October 5, the 3. Panzergrendier-Division was ordered to dispatch a small *Kampfgruppe* to the fort including four Jagdpanzer IV tank destroyers. At least two of these made their way into the fort by the following morning where they supported a counterattack by the newly arrived Füsilier-Kompanie 19. They were recalled to their parent unit that evening. By October 6, the German garrison had reached its peak strength of nine infantry companies, though many of these companies were well below strength.

The American attacks resumed on October 7, including an attempt to push a tank-infantry team down along one of the dry moats to attack the central fort. This attempt ended when an anti-tank gun knocked out the lead tank. Several pillboxes were captured in the southeast corner of the fort, but a German counterattack overran two platoons from Co. B/2nd Infantry including the company commander. The German garrison managed to move some small infantry guns into the fort, and fired them against the American infantry through the pillbox slits. The conditions on the surface of the fort were so lethal that most of the fighting degenerated into a nightmarish subterranean struggle. The fighting conditions inside the fort were hellish; there was no lighting in the tunnels and the air soon became choked by the frequent detonations of explosive charges. The surface fighting was equally deadly for the German infantry, and on October 7, the remnants of three

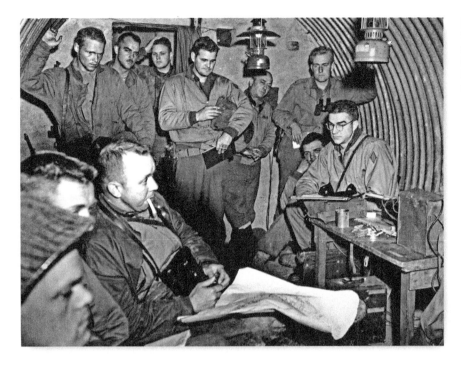

Brigadier-General Alan Warnock receives a briefing in a shelter near Fort Driant on October 10 shortly before his task force set out for the third series of attacks. (NARA)

infantry companies were sent out from the northern side of the fort in an attempt to move through the nearby woods and attack the American positions from the rear; the attack never materialized owing to casualties from artillery. Festung Metz also began steps to build up the defenses behind the fort on the presumption that the US Army would eventually try to surround the fort rather than continue a direct assault.

On the night of October 8–9, 3/2nd Infantry relieved 2/2nd Infantry and continued an effort to push along a narrow passageway in hopes of finally breaching one of the main gun casemates. An armored door blocked the key tunnel providing access to the southern gun casemate. A hole was blown in it but machinery and old cannons blocked the passage beyond. The door and the mechanical debris beyond were finally removed by the laborious and time-consuming means of acetylene torches. The next armored door was breached by a shaped charge, but the Germans quickly recovered and used the hole in the door for a machine gun. The 3/2nd Infantry created a baffle wall inside the tunnel which was defended by bazooka and machine-gun teams. German counter-mining efforts could be heard behind the concrete walls and around 1650hrs, October 9, a massive explosion occurred in the tunnel between the southern barracks on the southern-most gun casemate, abruptly halting the effort.

With the hopes for an easy victory evaporating, on October 9 a meeting was held in nearby Verdun including Major-Generals Walker, Irwin and Warnock, as well as Patton's chief of staff Maj. Gen. Hobart Gay. Warnock indicated that the fort could not be taken with available forces and that it would take at least four infantry battalions to surround the fort. Since the forces were not available, and in view of Eisenhower's moratorium, Gay instructed XX Corps to halt the operation. Gay later concluded that the attack might have succeeded had the initial attack been conducted by four battalions instead of one. The division withdrew Task Force Warnock on the night of October 12–13 after engineers had booby-trapped the escape route and demolished the areas that had been captured. About three tons of explosive were planted in various locations with fuses set at intervals ranging from 30 minutes to six hours to discourage German troops from following. The last US troops left Fort Driant at 2330hrs, October 12 and detonations inside the fort continued into the early morning hours of October 13.

American casualties in the attack were 798 including 64 killed, 547 wounded and 187 missing, about half of the attacking force. Six tanks were left behind in the fort out of the 16 taking part. Details of German casualties are lacking but were at least 400 men; there were barely 170 troops left in the fort by late October. Hauptmann August Weiler was decorated with the Knight's Cross for his leadership in the defense of Festung Driant, and Hitler personally authorized the creation of a "Metz" armband for the officer cadets who had so successfully resisted the American attacks along the Moselle front near Metz in September and early October 1944.

The 5th Division had the misfortune of attacking one of few forts of the Metz belt that was defended by a capable and steadfast garrison. Hauptmann Weiler later remarked that he "could not understand why the Americans chose to attack the strongest of the Metz forts that had always been considered impregnable." The Fort Driant fighting metastasized into a small-scale version of the nightmare that had enveloped the nearby Verdun forts three decades before. For Walker and XX Corps, the one clear lesson was that the old forts could not be dismissed in future attacks.

THE OCTOBER PAUSE

The fighting at Fort Driant was the most intense combat by Patton's Third Army in the XX Corps sector, but not the only fighting. Patton encouraged Walker to conduct small-scale operations to season new troops and to prevent complacency. The 90th Division on the vital Thionville–Metz road began a series of small-unit actions against the mining town of Maizières-les-Metz to secure a good line of departure for Operation *Madison*. The attacks on the

This is the central caserne of Fort Driant's infantry works, part of the main fort complex at the front of the complex. US troops never reached this area during the fighting. (NARA)

town began on October 3 by two infantry battalions and were slow going owing both to the small size of the attack force and the sturdy construction of the buildings in the town. Recognizing the importance of the town, AOK 1 reinforced it with Grenadier-Regiment 73 of the 19. Volksgrenadier-Division. Small-scale house-to-house fighting continued through October, but a Third Army freeze on the use of artillery ammunition over 3in., meaning all field artillery ammunition, limited the fighting after October 13. The division continued to use the town for training purposes at platoon and squad level through the middle of the month. On October 20, the fighting intensified after an M12 155mm self-propelled gun was used to blast the Hôtel de Ville (town hall) at point-blank range. With Third Army permission, the infantry attacks resumed in the hopes of securing the town before the onset of Operation *Madison*. A major attack on October 28 supported by 240mm howitzer fire finally overwhelmed the German defenses in the Hôtel de Ville, and the town was largely in American hands by October 30.

OPERATION *MADISON* BEGINS: XII CORPS

Eddy's XII Corps began the Operation *Madison* attack on November 8, a day before the attack in the neighboring XX Corps sector. There had been torrential rain on November 7, and the situation on the ground was so muddy that Eddy asked Patton to allow a day's delay. Patton's response was blunt: "Attack or name your replacement." The attack began at 0600hrs with an extensive artillery preparation that badly disrupted the forward German defenses. The attack won tactical surprise because of careful attention to camouflage when the three infantry divisions moved into their start positions the night before, and the miserable weather helped mask the preparations. The initial objectives, including key bridges, were mostly attained in the first day of attack.

On the right flank of the American attack, a regiment from the 361. Volksgrenadier-Division clung to Hill 310 (Côte Saint-Jean) overlooking the Seille River to the north of Moyenvic. This led to an intense three-day battle

TANK SKIRMISH AT GUÉBLING, NOVEMBER 14, 1944 (pp. 54–55)

The advance by the XII Corps on November 12–13 threatened to separate XIII SS-AK from the neighboring LXXXIX AK. Late on November 13, Generalleutnant Wend von Wietersheim, commander of the 11. Panzer-Division, decided to make another attempt at closing the gap by sending a reinforced *Kampfgruppe* from Panzergrenadier-Regiment 110, supported by Panther tanks from Panzer-Regiment 15 to attack from Guébling to Rodalbe. The German attack coincided with a push by the 4th Armored Division's Combat Command A (CCA) in the same sector. Task Force West of the CCA ran into the lead elements of the *Kampfgruppe* around 0845hrs on November 14 near the Kutzeling Farm outside Guébling and fought a six-hour battle trying to push past the German tanks. The surrounding fields were a muddy quagmire from the incessant rain and snow, and many roads were mined. With long fields of fire, the Panthers used their excellent long-range firepower to interdict the roads. At long range, the Panthers' frontal armor was impervious to the Sherman's 75mm and 76mm gun. Using

artillery spotter planes **(1)**, 155mm howitzers of the 191st Field Artillery Battalion began to shell them with both high explosive and smoke projectiles. The high explosive forced the German tankers to close their hatches and reduced their visibility. In the meantime, a platoon of tanks led by 1st Lieutenant Arthur L. Sell closed on the Panthers under the cover of the smoke. Sell had taken over command of Company A, 35th Tank Battalion, earlier when the company commander had been wounded. Sell's M4A3(76mm) tank **(2)** got to within 50 yards (45m) of the Panthers and engaged them against their thinner side and rear armor **(3)**. Sell managed to knock out two of the Panthers before his own tank became bogged in the mud. It was then hit at close range by fire from the Panthers, and two of his crew were killed and the other two wounded. In the meantime, two more tanks from Sell's platoon had maneuvered into place and knocked out the remaining Panthers. Sell was later awarded the Distinguished Service Cross for his actions that day.

for the hilltop against elements of the 26th Division and the hill was not captured until November 10. The fighting near Moyenvic began to force open a gap between the 361. and 559. Volksgrenadier-Divisionen which Eddy exploited by committing Combat Command A (CCA) of the 4th Armored Division. The tanks began to race up the Petite Seille River valley towards the Morhange road junction. The threat was so serious that Knobelsdorff committed the AOK 1 reserve, the 11. Panzer-Division, to stabilize the front. The divisional reconnaissance battalion supported by ten Panther tanks and a battalion of Panzergrenadier-Regiment 110 hit the 104th Infantry and CCA/4th Armored Division in the town of Rodalbe, halting the advance on November 12. Task Force Oden attempted to skirt around the defenses by an attack towards Guébling which overcame a tank force of about ten Panthers from the 11. Panzer-Division at the Kutzeling Farm, but suffered such heavy casualties from German artillery that it was ordered to withdraw. In the meantime, the 26th Division had continued its advance for the Koecking Ridge which eventually forced AOK 1 to begin to withdraw from this sector.

A similar tactic was used in the XII Corps center, which began with an attack by the 35th Division towards the woods northwest of Château-Salins, followed by a commitment of CCB/4th Armored Division once the initial German defense lines had been overcome on November 9. Another battle erupted with a *Kampfgruppe* of 11. Panzer-Division around Viviers. The steady but slow progress of the infantry of the 35th Division eventually forced a German withdrawal towards Morhange, and the fight for this critical road junction continued until it was finally taken on November 15.

The attack on the XII Corps left flank elicited the most violent German response. The Seille River in front of the 80th Division was badly swelled by the unusually heavy November rains, but by nightfall on November 8, the Americans had ten bridges over the river. The Delme Ridge was held by the 48. Infanterie-Division, with elements of SS-Panzergrenadier-Regiment 37 to the west. The 80th Division launched a two-regiment assault against the ridge

TOP

On November 11, a column of tanks trailed by an M4 (105mm) assault gun of the 15th Tank Battalion, 6th Armored Division, moves across the Seille River on a pontoon treadway bridge as divisional engineers check the bridge for problems. (NARA)

BOTTOM

The advance of Combat Command A (CCA) of the 4th Armored Division towards the Morhange road junction on November 12 forced Knobelsdorff to commit the AOK 1 reserve, the 11. Panzer-Division, to stabilize the front. This led to a bitter fight at the Kutzeling Farm near Guébling between Task Force Oden and about 10 Panthers from the 11. Panzer-Division. (NARA)

on November 9 which overcame the heavily fortified defenses by the end of the day. The success of the first two days of operations prompted Eddy to commit two combat commands of the 6th Armored Division to push ahead to the Nied Française River and then to the main corps objective of Faulquemont. In spite of the efforts expended by AOK 1 on the Delme Ridge defenses, the fighting in this sector soon became a pursuit by the 6th Armored Division, trying to prevent the battered 48. Infanterie-Division from reaching the new West-Stellung defense line on the Nied. The CCA/6th Armored Division secured a bridge at Hans-sur-Nied. This advance posed a major threat to XIII SS-AK and Knobelsdorff had no reserve to contest it since the 11. Panzer-Division was already entangled to the southeast. On November 11, Balck agreed to transfer the 36. Volksgrenadier-Division from the neighboring AOK 19 which could only slow but not stop the American advance because it arrived in a hasty and piecemeal fashion. The situation to the southeast of Metz was so dire that OB West finally agreed to transfer the 21. Panzer-Division back into Lorraine and Kampfgruppe Mühlen began to set up a defensive perimeter in the Forêt de Rémilly on November 13. Although the new reinforcements slowed the American advance, by November 15–16, the 80th Division was within artillery range of the Faulquemont road junction.

The first week of the XII Corps attack had succeeded in overcoming the German main line of resistance and had penetrated portions of the second defense line, the Nied-Stellung. After a short lull, Eddy intended to resume the attack on the right and center with an advance on the Saar River.

OPERATION *MADISON* BEGINS: XX CORPS

The XX Corps attack began a day later than the XII Corps on November 9 and was preceded by a "demonstration" by a regiment of the 95th Division near Uckange. Dubbed "Operation *Casanova*", this deception was intended to draw attention away from the main river-crossing operation by the 90th Division. The river crossing began shortly before midnight on November 8– 9. The main 90th Division attack consisted of two regiments landed by assault boats over the flooded Moselle in the pre-dawn hours of November 9. The early morning rain was so severe that German troops in the area were not on alert. Paradoxically, the flooding that impeded the US crossing efforts also flooded the extensive German minefields along the riverbank as well as many of the forward trench lines. The 359th Infantry landed near Malling,

The rains in November in Lorraine set a 30-year record. The extent of the flooding along the Moselle is evident in this view in Arnaville on November 10, with the downtown area flooded out. (NARA)

ABOVE
The bridging operations east of Thionville were complicated by the swollen state of the river which obliged the engineers to extend the pontoon treadway bridges for hundreds of additional yards in either direction. Here, Lt. Col. O. H. Robinson crosses one of the first completed bridges. (NARA)

RIGHT
The forts on either side of Thionville posed a substantial problem in the river-crossing operations as many sites were pre-registered by the fort's artillery batteries. This was the case with the existing bridges in Thionville as seen at this bridge that was hit again during the fighting on November 17. (NARA)

captured the garrison and moved swiftly down the road to Kerling where the German position was rushed and overwhelmed. The neighboring 358th Infantry landed and advanced past Fort Koenigsmacker in the dark, leaving two companies to deal with the fort. Companies A and B, 358th Infantry, quickly cut through the outer wire belts and reached the defensive trenches before being discovered. The infantry was accompanied by a platoon of the 315th Engineer Combat Battalion, which supervised the systematic attack on observation domes using satchel charges and gasoline. Although the infantry in the fort was subjected to mortar fire, the garrison from Grenadier-Regiment 74, 19. Volksgrenadier-Division, only made one sally out of the shelters which was crushed. By the end of the day, the two companies controlled the western side of the fort, and additional explosives had to be flown in to continue the demolition efforts. The fort's artillery continued to bombard the river landing sites, delaying the erection of bridges. By the end of the first day's attack, the 90th Division had eight infantry battalions across the river but had not yet run into the MLR further south.

German resistance came mainly from artillery, and the force that landed over the Moselle was soon isolated by the river which continued to swell due to the previous few days' rain. Persistent German artillery prevented the erection of bridges, and the river flow soon became too swift and turbulent for assault boats. The German infantry in this sector was so poor that Balck had ordered the divisional commanders to avoid counterattacking the first waves of US infantry and instead to use artillery and pre-positioned machine-gun nests to halt the attacks. With the 11. Panzer-Division committed further south in the XII Corps sector, Balck contacted Berlin to plead for reinforcements. Two battalions of the 25. Panzergrenadier-Division were dispatched, but became stuck due to transportation problems. Instead, an infantry company from Grenadier-Regiment 59, 19. Volksgrenadier-Division, was sent towards Kerling in the pre-dawn hours of November 12, supported by three assault guns, which overran outposts of the 359th Infantry before being stopped. The 90th Division foothold over the Moselle remained precarious through November 10 as the Moselle had continued to flood and the inundated areas near the crossing points were between 1,000 and 2,000 yards wide (900–1,800m). The infantry continued to assault Fort Koenigsmacker, and the first attempts were made to silence the small Maginot fortifications of the Métrich group. Fortunately, the 19. Volksgrenadier-Division had no reserves for a counterattack and a bridge was completed near the Malling crossing site around midnight, allowing supplies and reinforcements to flow over the river.

The dominating position of Fort Koenigsmacker to the Moselle River crossing sites forced the 90th Division to stage an attack on it starting on November 9. Garrisoned by units of Grenadier-Regiment 74, the fort was assaulted by the 1/358th Infantry and the garrison finally surrendered on November 11. The small village of Basse-Ham can be seen in the background. (MHI)

EVENTS

1 The 359th Infantry departs Gavisse area in assault boats at 0330hrs, November 9, and lands near Malling, capturing most of 6./GR 713.

2 359th Infantry attacks and occupies Kerling which was garrisoned by construction troops of 4./Bau Battalion 3.

3 The 1/358th Infantry departs Cattenom at 0330hrs, November 9, and lands west of Basse-Ham.

4 Cos. A and B, 358th Infantry, cut through the outer wire belts of Fort Koenigsmacher and reached the defensive trenches before being discovered. The infantry was accompanied by a platoon of the 315th Engineer Combat Battalion, which supervised the systematic attack on observation domes and armored doors using satchel charges and gasoline.

5 The Moselle River continues to swell and flood banks from a normal width of 350 to 2,400ft (105–730m). Rains continue, and the velocity of the water greatly impedes traffic over river.

6 Attempts to construct bridges at Cattenom are frustrated by rising water and artillery fire from Fort Koenigsmacher, which destroys the first five truckloads of bridging equipment.

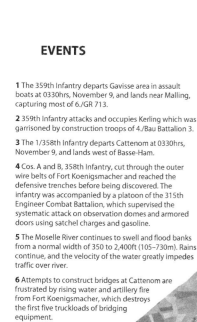

7 First attempt to assemble footbridge Moselle at Malling frustrated by German mortar fire. The 206th Engineer Combat Battalion instead set up two ferries. Another infantry support bridge about three-quarters finished was lost at 1100hrs, November 9, when accidently struck by a raft.

8 At 0300hrs, November 10, a *Kampfgruppe* of Volksgrenadier-Regiment 59 including 1./VGR 59, two anti-tank rocket platoons of 14./VRG 59 and three StuG IIIs of StuG-Batallion 25 hit 3/359th in Kerling. As fighting continues, two other companies of VGR 59 enter the fight and two US rifle companies pushed out of town.

9 At 0630hrs, November 10, 3/357th Infantry moves out of assembly area to assault Maginot forts around Metrich.

10 Co. C, 358th Infantry, reinforces assault on Fort Koenigsmacker. Due to river conditions, more explosives air-dropped to assault teams on fort using five artillery spotter planes. Casernes attacked using gasoline poured into ventilation shafts.

11 During November 10, two companies from VGR 1216 sent from Mazières-les-Metz to reinforce Fort Yutz and Thionville. Another company sent to Fort Illange.

12 On November 10, river reaches over 8,000ft (2,400m) wide, flooding towns of Cattenom and Gavisse. River finally crests at 1800hrs, November 11.

13 The 991st Treadway Bridge Company finally assembles a bridge at Malling at 0200hrs November 11, but swollen river is 6ft deep at access points, preventing use until midnight November 11–12 after water finally begins to recede.

14 The 2/357th Infantry joins 3/357th Infantry on November 11 in assault of Maginot forts in the Metrich area.

15 A German attempt to relieve Fort Koenigsmacher is foiled when a prisoner reveals the march route. An alarm company is ambushed by Co. K, 358th Infantry, and 145 men killed or captured.

16 Relentless assault against casemates on November 11 finally forces German garrison in fort to attempt break-out attempt. They run into Co. G, 358th Infantry, and are forced to surrender. A total of 372 prisoners-of-war are captured at the fort including the battalion headquarters of I./GR 74, a company of infantry from GR 74, most of Füsilier-Kompanie 19, and troops of two alarm companies.

17 The 2/378th Infantry move across the Moselle on November 11 to begin reduction of Thionville.

18 Company F, 378th Infantry, is reinforced to assault Fort Yutz on November 12 which is held by elements of GR 74 and VGR 1216.

19 At 0300hrs on November 13, a *Kampfgruppe* from I./Panzergrenadier-Regiment 35 with ten tanks and assault guns attempts to roll up the 90th Division bridgehead from the 359th Infantry sector. Although the attack does recapture Kerling for a time, in the end it is routed at a cost of over 400 dead, 150 prisoners, four tanks and five assault guns. Its remnants withdraw and III./Panzergrenadier-Regiment eventually arrives in Distroff area over the following days.

20 Co. F/378th Infantry assaults Fort Illange on November 14, which is cleared by November 15.

21 On the afternoon of November 14, Combat Command A, 10th Armored Division moves the Moselle over the Malling bridges.

22 On the afternoon of November 14, Combat Command B, 10th Armored Division, moves over Moselle at the Cattenom bridges.

XX CORPS CROSSES THE MOSELLE AT THIONVILLE, NOVEMBER 9–14, 1944

US forces break through the German defenses on the Moselle

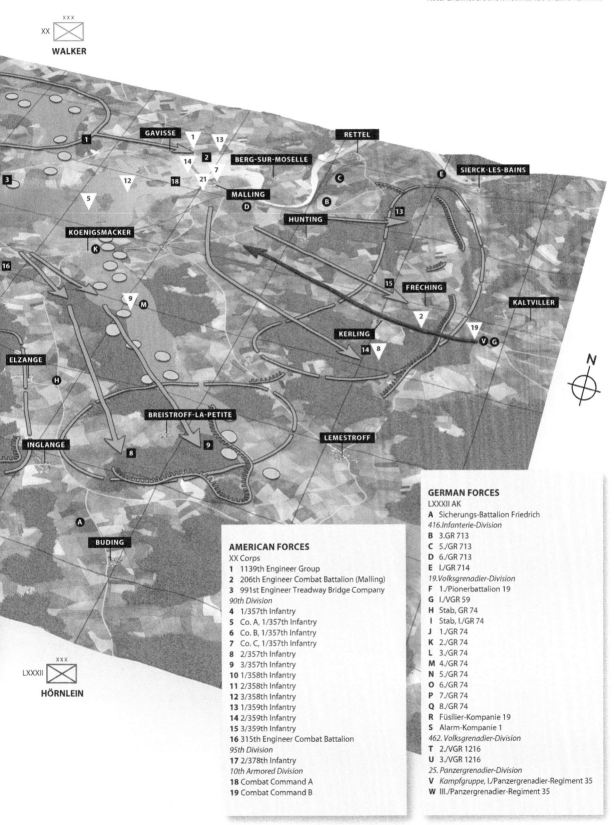

Note: Gridlines are shown at intervals of 2km/1.24miles

XX ⊠ XXX
WALKER

GAVISSE
RETTEL
BERG-SUR-MOSELLE
SIERCK-LES-BAINS
MALLING
HUNTING
KOENIGSMACKER
FRÉCHING
KALTVILLER
KERLING
ELZANGE
BREISTROFF-LA-PETITE
LEMESTROFF
INGLANGE
BUDING

LXXXII ⊠ XXX
HÖRNLEIN

AMERICAN FORCES
XX Corps
1 1139th Engineer Group
2 206th Engineer Combat Battalion (Malling)
3 991st Engineer Treadway Bridge Company
90th Division
4 1/357th Infantry
5 Co. A, 1/357th Infantry
6 Co. B, 1/357th Infantry
7 Co. C, 1/357th Infantry
8 2/357th Infantry
9 3/357th Infantry
10 1/358th Infantry
11 2/358th Infantry
12 3/358th Infantry
13 1/359th Infantry
14 2/359th Infantry
15 3/359th Infantry
16 315th Engineer Combat Battalion
95th Division
17 2/378th Infantry
10th Armored Division
18 Combat Command A
19 Combat Command B

GERMAN FORCES
LXXXII AK
A Sicherungs-Battalion Friedrich
416.Infanterie-Division
B 3.GR 713
C 5./GR 713
D 6./GR 713
E I./GR 714
19.Volksgrenadier-Division
F 1./Pionerbattalion 19
G I./VGR 59
H Stab, GR 74
I Stab, I./GR 74
J 1./GR 74
K 2./GR 74
L 3./GR 74
M 4./GR 74
N 5./GR 74
O 6./GR 74
P 7./GR 74
Q 8./GR 74
R Füsilier-Kompanie 19
S Alarm-Kompanie 1
462. Volksgrenadier-Division
T 2./VGR 1216
U 3./VGR 1216
25. Panzergrenadier-Division
V *Kampfgruppe*, I./Panzergrenadier-Regiment 35
W III./Panzergrenadier-Regiment 35

The 19. Volksgrenadier-Division attempted to reinforce Fort Koenigsmacker on November 11, but the company was ambushed. The fort garrison attempted to break out afterwards, but was caught in the open and some 372 troops were forced to surrender. German counterattacks intensified that day, but the establishment of a bridge over the Moselle ensured a steady flow of supplies and reinforcements; the Moselle floodtide began to recede, and the main German fortifications in the foreground including Koenigsmacker and Metrich had fallen.

The counterattack by a *Kampfgruppe* from Panzergrenadier-Regiment 35 with ten tanks and assault guns finally struck south of Sierck in the early afternoon of November 13 and attempted to roll up the 90th Division bridgehead from the 359th Infantry sector, once again directed towards Kerling. Although the attack did create some inroads into the US defense, in the end it was routed at a cost of over 400 dead, 150 prisoners, four tanks and five assault guns.

In an effort to solidify the bridgehead over the Moselle enough to permit the deployment of the 10th Armored Division, steps began to expand the 95th Division "demonstration" into a functional bridgehead by clearing out forts near Thionville that covered the Thionville–Metz highway. The old Vauban-era Fort Yutz was quickly overcome, but the garrison of Fort Illange (Feste Illangen) resisted. The fort was reduced by artillery and an assault by 2/377th Infantry, which forced the garrison's surrender on November 15.

The 1/377th Infantry was hit by an intense 19. Volksgrenadier-Division counterattack near its bridgehead on November 14, but finally pushed away from the river by the afternoon. The 95th Division forces over the Moselle were formed into Task Force Bacon on November 15, consisting of two infantry battalions, two tank destroyer companies, a company of tanks and supporting troops. With the bridgehead secure and enough tactical bridging erected, the two combat commands of the 10th Armored Division began moving out on the afternoon of November 15. The road network was far from ideal for a mechanized force, and the combat commands quickly broke up into more convenient task forces to move over the Nied River and begin the operations towards the Saar.

An M10 from a tank destroyer battalion of Patton's Third US Army near Fort Koenigsmacker in the Metz defensive belt on November 21, 1944. This unit was supporting the 90th Division and Task Force Bacon during the final assault on Metz, where resistance finally collapsed the next day, November 22, after having held out for almost two months. This vehicle appears to have an armored roof fitted over the rear of the turret, but it is obscured by the tarp.

The river-crossing operations near Thionville were threatened by the four small forts of Feste Illangen on the Illange Plateau because they had good observation of the crossing sites. The forts were weakly held by a garrison from Grenadier-Regiment 74 and were subjected to a heavy artillery bombardment followed by a close assault by 2/378th Infantry using explosive charges on November 15 leading to the surrender of the forts. This view of the forts is looking towards the east with Thionville to the far left beyond this view. (MHI)

In spite of the threat posed by the 10th Armored Division advance, AOK 1 decided to use its sole counterattack force, the *Kampfgruppe* from Panzergrenadier-Regiment 35, to try to stop the 90th Division advance. Around daybreak on November 15, the *Kampfgruppe*, reinforced by infantry from Grenadier-Regiment 74 of the 19. Volksgrenadier-Division, hit the 2/358th Infantry in the town of Distroff. After a preliminary artillery barrage, the Panzer-infantry attack broke into the town, leading to a four-hour mêlée that finally ended in a German withdrawal. German losses included four tanks, four StuG III assault guns, and 16 half-tracks along with at least 150 dead. This was the last major German counterattack in this sector owing to dwindling resources.

The forts in this sector continued to impede the advance on Metz. As the 90th Division continued its southward advance, the lead regiment was repeatedly hit by 75mm fire from the neighboring Maginot Line fort near Hackenberg. The fort was hit by counter-battery fire, close-range tank destroyer fire and even 240mm howitzers, all to no avail. That evening, a section of M12 155mm GMCs was moved up close to the fort and began an accurate close-range shelling that finally silenced the fort's guns

The continued 90th Division drive south and the lack of reserves forced Balck to decide whether to risk losing both the 19. Volksgrenadier-Division and 416. Infanterie-Division or withdraw them east to the Saar while there was still a chance. Balck was well aware of the lack of consensus about the fate of Metz in Berlin. Rundstedt and the OB West headquarters had been arguing for an abandonment of the city in favor of establishing a firm defense line along the Westwall. Keitel, reflecting Hitler's adamant refusal to abandon Metz, instructed Balck to hold on to the city "to the last man." Balck wanted the Metz garrison to tie down the advancing American units as long as possible but decided to leave it to fight to the end on its own rather than lose most of the north wing of AOK 1 in an encirclement. On the night of November 17, AOK 1 was instructed to begin to pull both divisions out of their defensive positions and to withdraw to the Nied-Stellung to the east. By this stage of the campaign, the American 90th Division had suffered 2,300 casualties but had taken 2,100 prisoners and destroyed or captured 40 tanks and assault guns, 75 field guns and inflicted substantial losses on three German divisions.

The 5th Infantry Division along the Seille River southwest of Metz launched its attack on November 9, a day after the 80th Division in the neighboring XII Corps sector. The division was instructed to avoid the Metz

fortification belt and instead to push eastward to sever the main roads leading into Metz. The initial attack faced a great deal of flooding along the Seille River, but not to the extent of the 90th Division to the north. Equally important, the defenses of the 17. SS-Panzergrenadier Division had been badly disrupted by the earlier XII Corps attack, and the 2nd Infantry, 5th Infantry Division, was able to follow behind the rapid exploitation of CCB, 6th Armored Division. In the face of weak opposition the 5th Infantry Division engineers erected a treadway bridge over the Nied-Française. This elicited the first strong counterattack in this sector by a *Kampfgrupppe* of SS-Panzergrenadier-Regiment 38 and the 21. Panzer Division but the 2nd Infantry beat it off. While the 2nd Infantry held the division's right flank, the other two regiments pushed on to envelop Metz. German resistance intensified as the division reached the outskirts of the city, including an attempt by SS-Panzergrenadier-Regiment 38 to seize the Sanry Bridge.

On November 13, the 17. SS-Panzergrenadier-Division, supported by the 21. Panzer-Division, staged a major counterattack against the Sanry bridgehead of the 2nd Infantry. The bridgehead was pounded by all available divisional artillery during the morning and early afternoon, and the main attacks began in the mid-afternoon by Panzergrenadier-Regiment 192. The attacks continued into the night, with the US troops forced back into the town itself. The final attacks were staged early on November 14, but finally petered out after the attacking forces had lost about 500 men. As a result, Kampfgruppe von Matzdorf, based on SS-Panzergrenadier-Regiment 38, organized a blocking position on the eastern side of Metz. The four *Festungs-MG-Bataillone* in this sector were subordinated to this *Kampfgruppe*.

THE BATTLE FOR METZ

On November 11, AOK 1 gave orders to begin the evacuation of Metz by non-essential personnel. The city contained a large number of administrative personnel who began moving east. Hitler also indicated that he did not want the 17. SS-Panzergrenadier-Division caught in the Metz pocket. Holding "Festung Metz" was the 462. Volksgrenadier-Division, the city's former depot training division. The elite officer candidates had departed nearly a month earlier, and the division was fleshed out with overage troops and those with physical and medical problems. A number of *Festungs-MG-Bataillone* and other fortification units were moved forward from the Westwall and put at

The encirclement of Metz, November 9–19

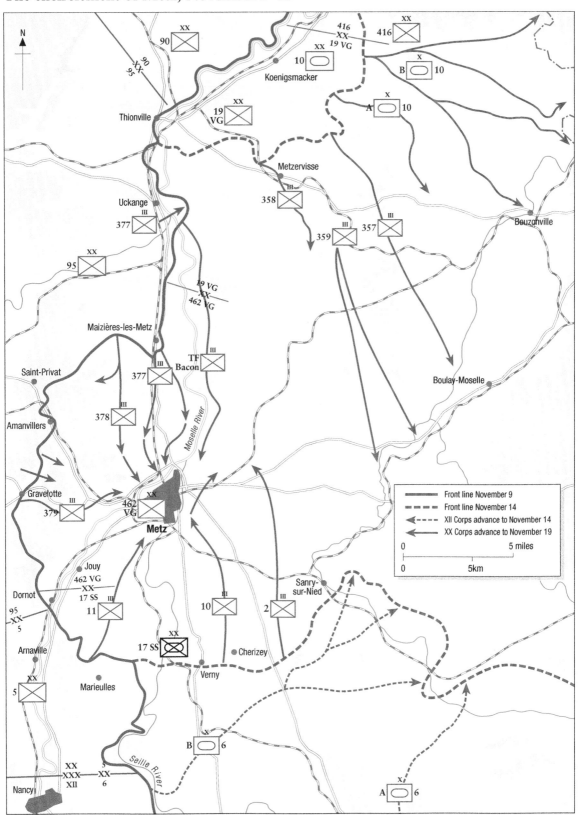

the division's disposal; it was renamed "Festungs-Division Metz" as a result. After Gen.Lt. Vollrath Luebbe suffered a stroke on November 12 command fell to Generalleutnant Heinrich Kittel, a Russian Front veteran and urban defense specialist. Kittel was disturbed to learn that some 1,700 troops were tied up in the Metz forts and ordered the garrisons reduced to skeleton crews; this order was widely ignored by local commanders who recognized the value of such defenses when relying on such poor-quality infantry.

While the 5th Division was making the surge towards Metz from the southeast, the 95th Division was pushing down from the north past Maizières. By November 14, American patrols were probing the outer Metz defenses from the northwest, west, and the southeast. The fighting had proceeded rapidly enough that the 95th Division contacted Walker at XX Corps headquarters to request a change of plans. Instead of waiting until the 5th and 90th Division had completely sealed off the city, the division wanted to proceed immediately to attack into Metz. The division had its three regiments in line, approaching the northwest quadrant of the city.

The 377th Infantry was approaching the city from the north in parallel with Task Force Bacon on the eastern side of the Moselle. TF Bacon consisted of the 1/377th Infantry and 2/378th Infantry reinforced with tanks, tank destroyers and a pair of M12 155mm GMCs. Further to the west, the 378th Infantry began attacks against the critical Feves Ridge. Kampfgruppe Stössel held this sector of the Metz defenses.

A column of the 1/378th Infantry, 95th Division, supported by M4A3 tanks of the 735th Tank Battalion enters the northwestern suburbs of Metz on November 17. (NARA)

EVENTS

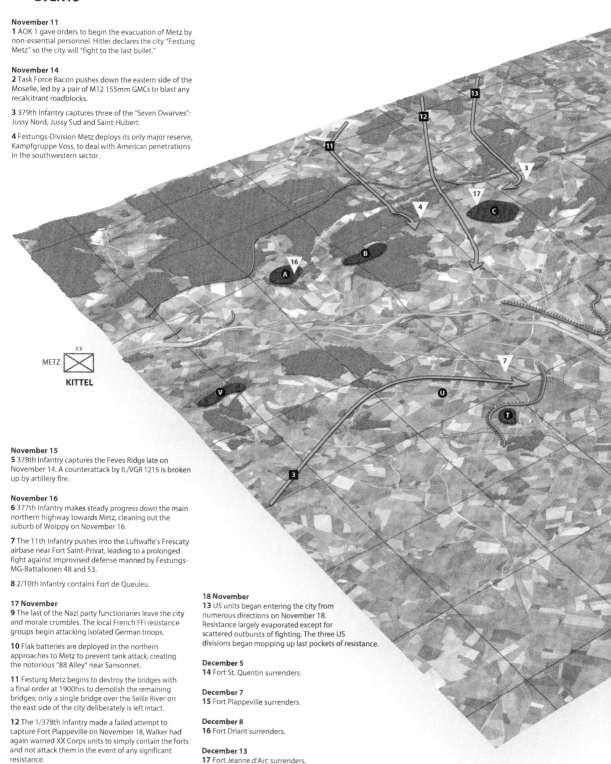

November 11
1 AOK 1 gave orders to begin the evacuation of Metz by non-essential personnel. Hitler declares the city "Festung Metz" so the city will "fight to the last bullet."

November 14
2 Task Force Bacon pushes down the eastern side of the Moselle, led by a pair of M12 155mm GMCs to blast any recalcitrant roadblocks.

3 379th Infantry captures three of the "Seven Dwarves": Jussy Nord, Jussy Sud and Saint-Hubert.

4 Festungs-Division Metz deploys its only major reserve, Kampfgruppe Voss, to deal with American penetrations in the southwestern sector.

November 15
5 378th Infantry captures the Feves Ridge late on November 14. A counterattack by II./VGR 1215 is broken up by artillery fire.

November 16
6 377th Infantry makes steady progress down the main northern highway towards Metz, cleaning out the suburb of Woippy on November 16.

7 The 11th Infantry pushes into the Luftwaffe's Frescaty airbase near Fort Saint-Privat, leading to a prolonged fight against improvised defense manned by Festungs-MG-Battalionen 48 and 53.

8 2/10th Infantry contains Fort de Queuleu.

17 November
9 The last of the Nazi party functionaries leave the city and morale crumbles. The local French FFI resistance groups begin attacking isolated German troops.

10 Flak batteries are deployed in the northern approaches to Metz to prevent tank attack, creating the notorious "88 Alley" near Sansonnet.

11 Festung Metz begins to destroy the bridges with a final order at 1900hrs to demolish the remaining bridges; only a single bridge over the Seille River on the east side of the city deliberately is left intact.

12 The 1/378th Infantry made a failed attempt to capture Fort Plappeville on November 18, Walker had again warned XX Corps units to simply contain the forts and not attack them in the event of any significant resistance.

18 November
13 US units began entering the city from numerous directions on November 18. Resistance largely evaporated except for scattered outbursts of fighting. The three US divisions began mopping up last pockets of resistance.

December 5
14 Fort St. Quentin surrenders.

December 7
15 Fort Plappeville surrenders.

December 8
16 Fort Driant surrenders.

December 13
17 Fort Jeanne d'Arc surrenders.

METZ XX KITTEL

BATTLE FOR METZ, NOVEMBER 14–19, 1944
US forces surround Metz and fight their way through the defenses, taking the city

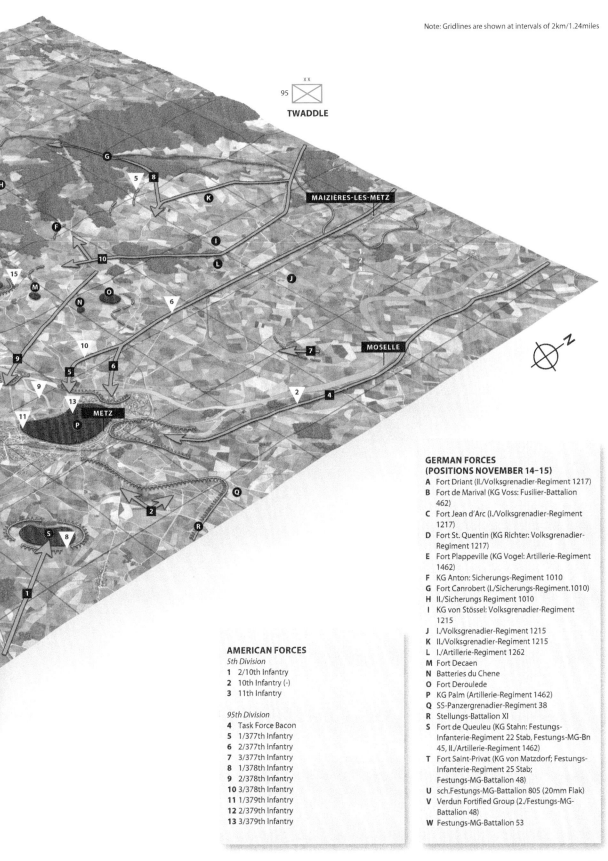

Note: Gridlines are shown at intervals of 2km/1.24miles

95 XX ⊠ TWADDLE

MAIZIÈRES-LES-METZ

MOSELLE

METZ

N↗

AMERICAN FORCES

5th Division
1 2/10th Infantry
2 10th Infantry (-)
3 11th Infantry

95th Division
4 Task Force Bacon
5 1/377th Infantry
6 2/377th Infantry
7 3/377th Infantry
8 1/378th Infantry
9 2/378th Infantry
10 3/378th Infantry
11 1/379th Infantry
12 2/379th Infantry
13 3/379th Infantry

GERMAN FORCES
(POSITIONS NOVEMBER 14–15)
A Fort Driant (II./Volksgrenadier-Regiment 1217)
B Fort de Marival (KG Voss: Fusilier-Battalion 462)
C Fort Jean d'Arc (I./Volksgrenadier-Regiment 1217)
D Fort St. Quentin (KG Richter: Volksgrenadier-Regiment 1217)
E Fort Plappeville (KG Vogel: Artillerie-Regiment 1462)
F KG Anton: Sicherungs-Regiment 1010
G Fort Canrobert (I./Sicherungs-Regiment.1010)
H II./Sicherungs Regiment 1010
I KG von Stössel: Volksgrenadier-Regiment 1215
J I./Volksgrenadier-Regiment 1215
K II./Volksgrenadier-Regiment 1215
L I./Artillerie-Regiment 1262
M Fort Decaen
N Batteries du Chene
O Fort Deroulede
P KG Palm (Artillerie-Regiment 1462)
Q SS-Panzergrenadier-Regiment 38
R Stellungs-Battalion XI
S Fort de Queuleu (KG Stahn: Festungs-Infanterie-Regiment 22 Stab, Festungs-MG-Bn 45, II./Artillerie-Regiment 1462)
T Fort Saint-Privat (KG von Matzdorf; Festungs-Infanterie-Regiment 25 Stab; Festungs-MG-Battalion 48)
U sch.Festungs-MG-Battalion 805 (20mm Flak)
V Verdun Fortified Group (2./Festungs-MG-Battalion 48)
W Festungs-MG-Battalion 53

The third regiment of the 95th Division, the 379th Infantry, was attacking from the west. This sector was defended by Kampfgruppe Richter based on Volksgrenadier-Regiment 1217. However, the main challenge in this area was the heavy concentration of Mosel-Stellung forts, including some of the most active such as Forts Driant and Jeanne d'Arc. Walker and XX Corps had made it explicitly clear that a direct attack on the main forts was to be avoided, so the tactical approach in this sector was to infiltrate past the main forts by passing through the "Seven Dwarfs." This was a series of small forts that had been constructed by the German Army in 1917 to fill gaps in the Metz fortification belt. Many of the small forts were weakly held if at all, and, on November 14, the 378th Infantry captured three of these in the face of little opposition. The response from the thinly stretched Kampfgruppe Richter was feeble. As a result, Kittel assigned his only major reserve, Kampfgruppe Voss based on the division's reconnaissance unit, Füsilier-

Bataillon 462. No sooner was this unit under way by truck from the city to the southwestern sector than reports began to filter in from the north that the 378th Infantry had captured the Feves Ridge. A pre-dawn counterattack by II./ Kampfgruppe Stössel was broken up by US artillery fire. Kittel was told that no reserves were available from LXXXII AK, so he turned to Knobelsdorff at AOK 1 in the afternoon. Permission was granted to use SS-Panzergrenadier-Regiment 38, but this was a hollow offer considering that the unit had been badly decimated in the fighting with the US 5th Infantry Division for the Sanry bridgehead, and, more importantly, it was the mainstay of the defense on the other side of the city near the Bois de l'Hôpital. The southeastern sector was itself the subject of continuing attacks by elements of the US 5th Infantry Division which were bumping into the inner ring of forts by the afternoon of November 15. In the end, only a single Waffen-SS company was sent by truck to the threatened northern sector. Although Kittel had arranged for a number of coordinated counterattacks on the advancing American forces on November 15, none proved possible though there were numerous local counterattacks. The seizure of Fort de Feves on the critical Feves Ridge led to a vigorous counterattack by II./Volksgrenadier-Regiment 1215. This particular fort was not especially powerful in terms of artillery, but it served as an excellent observation post for directing German artillery against the approaching 95th Division, and its capture led to an immediate degradation in German firepower in the northern sector. The 377th Infantry

A rifle squad from the 95th Division patrols for snipers inside Metz on November 20, 1944. (NARA)

BELOW
US troops advance through the outskirts of Metz. Behind the GI is an M8 light armored car and an abandoned 88mm PaK 43/41 anti-tank gun. (NARA)

made steady progress down the main northern highway towards Metz, cleaning out the suburb of Woippy on November 16. Attempts to push south of Woippy ran into the forts covering this approach, especially Fort Deroulede and Fort Gambetta, and efforts to seize the forts were brusquely rebuffed by heavy fire from the forts.

The attacks by the 379th Infantry against the heavily fortified western sector bogged down in the face of intense artillery fire from the neighboring forts as well as vigorous counterattacks by Kampfgruppe Voss and other units in the sector. The erosion of the Metz defenses in the north was also matched in the south. The 11th Infantry had pushed up behind the forts along the Moselle and by November 16 was pushing into the Luftwaffe's Frescaty airbase near Fort Saint-Privat. This base had numerous shelters and buildings that had been fortified as improvised defense points by Festungs-MG-Bataillonen 48 and 53.

The advance by TF Bacon on the east side of the Moselle helped to isolate the city from any reinforcements coming from the east. On November 16, TF Bacon had pushed more than 4 miles (7km) by using the heavy firepower of its pair of attached M12 self-propelled guns to blast any obstinate roadblocks. Standing in the way was Fort Saint-Julien which was assaulted on the morning of November 18. Festungs-Bataillon St. Julien attempted to defend from the outlying town before withdrawing into the fort. The fighting continued for most of the day, with the M12 self-propelled guns finally convincing the garrison to surrender. The neighboring garrison in Fort Bellecroix set a time charge in the ammunition depot inside the fort before surrendering to the 377th Infantry, blowing the old fort apart.

By November 17, the end of Festung Metz seemed near. The last of the Nazi party functionaries left that day, and rumors began to circulate that American tanks had entered the suburbs. The first white bed sheets began flying from houses, and the local Forces Françaises de l'Intérieur (FFI) resistance groups became emboldened and began seizing guns from isolated German troops. An effort was made to evacuate German civilians using

Troops of the 101st Infantry, 26th Division, escort German emissaries under a flag of truce during the surrender of Fort Jeanne d'Arc (Feste Kaiserin) on December 13. This provides a good view of the size of the casernes in these forts. (NARA)

military police, and convoys escorted by eight military police companies began exiting the city. By the end of the day, the situation in Metz and in the rest of AOK 1 seemed so ominous that Knobelsdorff again contacted Balck to request permission to abandon Metz and to permit a general withdrawal towards the Westwall. Since Hitler had classified the city as "Festung Metz" such a decision, regardless of its tactical soundness, was politically unacceptable. Regardless of Balck's refusal, on November 17, Knobelsdorff sent Kittel a teletype message informing him that AOK 1 would be breaking off from the city and that Festung Metz would now be on its own. Berlin had informed Balck that Hitler did not want 17. SS-Panzergrenadier-Division trapped in the Metz pocket, and on the night of November 16–17, Panzergrenadier-Regiment 38 and other elements of the division near Metz withdrew to the northeast without bothering to inform Kittel. On discovering their withdrawal, Kittel attempted to organize improvised alarm companies to reinforce the abandoned eastern defenses from about 700 stragglers held in the center of the city. With no reliable officers or NCOs, this effort evaporated. Remaining anti-aircraft guns were repositioned to serve as improvised anti-tank defenses at major intersections, and the main north–south route into the city near Sansonnet was soon dubbed "88 Alley" by American troops owing to the number of Flak guns located there.

With all four columns of the 95th Division within reach of the city from the west and north, and with two regiments of the 5th Division within range from the southeast, on November 17 Walker decided to start the final push into Metz itself. Orders were sent out that a coordinated attack would begin at 1400hrs on November 17 with an initial aim to race to major bridges in the hopes of securing them prior to German demolition. French liaison officers in XX Corps headquarters also contacted the FFI unit in Metz, numbering about 400 members, in hopes that they might disrupt any German attempts to sabotage the bridges. The Germans were likely to demolish the bridges, so XX Corps engineers moved assault boats to the Moselle and Seille for improvised crossings.

Troops from the 101st Infantry, 26th Division, move along the top of one of the casernes at Fort Jeanne d'Arc during the surrender on December 13. This gives a good impression of the depth of the dry moats at these forts, highlighting the difficulty of infantry and tank assaults against them. (NARA)

The assistant commander of the 26th Division, Brig. Gen. Harlan Hartness, accepts the surrender of the garrison of Fort Jeanne d'Arc (Feste Kaiserin) on December 13, the last of the Metz forts to succumb to the siege. (NARA)

Kittel had already begun to demolish the bridges days before to prevent any last-minute confusion and he sent out orders on the evening of November 17 at 1900hrs to destroy the remaining bridges; this was carried out through the early morning hours of November 18. In one case, a patrol from 3/378th Infantry reached the bridge before its detonation, but the charge was set off while they were on the bridge killing eight men. Only a single bridge over the Seille River on the east side of the city deliberately was left intact. One unexpected consequence of the order was that when one of the bridges connecting to Ile Chambière was demolished, it also severed the main cable link between the headquarters and the army telephone exchange connected to all the forts. As a result, Kittel lost all contact with his scattered units except for limited radio and courier contacts. One consequence of relying on the forts was that a large portion of the Metz garrison was essentially trapped in the final days and not able to participate in the last of the fighting. After the 1/378th Infantry made a failed attempt to capture Fort Plappeville on November 18, Walker had again warned XX Corps units simply to contain the forts and not attack them in the event of any significant resistance.

US units began entering the city from numerous directions on November 18, and resistance largely evaporated except for scattered outbursts of shooting. The US divisions began mopping up the last pockets of resistance, and Gen.Lt. Kittel was found in an underground hospital after he had been wounded during the street fighting.

Walker instructed the units of XX Corps not to assault the remaining forts, but to keep them isolated with small containment forces. Walker was determined to avoid unnecessary casualties and did not want to waste artillery ammunition for the ensuing Saar River campaign. From prisoner interrogations, it was evident that the forts were demoralized and short of water and food. They began to succumb to hunger: Fort Saint-Quentin on December 5, followed by Plappeville on December 7, Driant on December 8, and the final holdout, Jeanne d'Arc on December 13. These forts contained more than 2,200 troops on their surrender.

ON TO THE SAAR: XII CORPS

The German predicament in Lorraine paled in comparison with the events in Alsace to the south. Heeresgrupe G had tended to favor AOK 1 in Lorraine since the natural defenses and fortifications in Alsace were judged so much more substantial. Access to the "Burgundy Gate" had traditionally been up through the Belfort Gap along the Rhine plain past a string of fortified cities including Neuf Brisach, Belfort and Mulhouse. This narrow avenue was heavily fortified and mined. The Rhine plain in Alsace was protected on the western side by the Vosges Mountains which had frustrated attackers for centuries. When finally assaulted by the 6th Army Group as part of the November 1944 offensives, the AOK 19 defenses crumbled in a rapid and alarming fashion. The French First Army pushed up through the Belfort Gap and reached the Rhine on November 22. Even more surprisingly, the Seventh US Army quickly overcame the Vosges defense lines and emerged from the mountains through the Saverne Gap, snatching the provincial capital of Strasbourg on the run. This later action had direct implications for Patton's Third US Army since it abutted the sector of the XII Corps. In view of the disaster in Alsace, Heeresgruppe G had even fewer reserves to allot to the troubled AOK 1.

In spite of the obvious weakening of the German defenses in the AOK 1 sector, Patton's Third US Army had its own problems. The most significant was its diminishing infantry strength. This was all the more critical owing to weather-induced problems with airpower and armor. The continual rainy and snowy weather, combined with the diversion of much of Ninth Air Force's strength further north to the high-priority First US Army sector, deprived

This Panzerjäger 38(t) Ausf. M Marder III tank destroyer of Panzerjäger Abteilung 61 of 11. Panzer-Division was knocked out in the fighting with the 6th Armored Division on November 22, 1944, near Saint-Jean Rohrbach. (NARA)

The Lorraine Offensive, November 8 to December 19, 1944

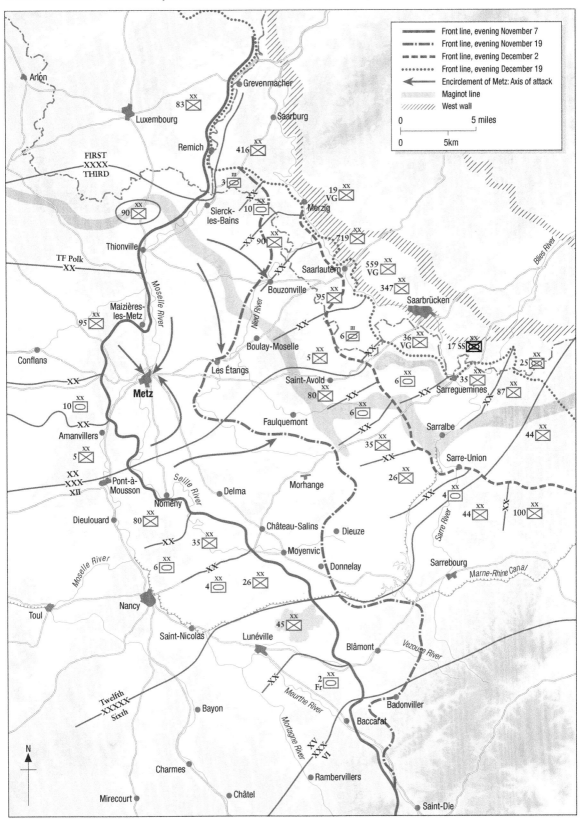

Patton's forces of extensive air support for much of the month. Equally critical, the wet and muddy ground conditions severely constrained mobile mechanized operations. Tanks could not operate off the road network because of the morass of mud in the fields, leading to a front that was "one tank wide." Tank operations were often confined to hard roads, and these narrow avenues were easy to defend using mines and anti-tank weapons.

As a result, infantry played the central role in the autumn 1944 fighting in Lorraine. Infantry losses were high owing to the intensity of the combat, but medical casualties soon equaled or exceeded combat casualties. The US Army was not well prepared for the onset of a wet winter particularly with regard to proper footwear, and the rainy and cold conditions with rain alternating with snow and sleet led to an escalating problem with trench foot. On top of this, the US Army had underestimated the dynamics of casualty replacement, and infantry replacements had largely run out by mid-autumn. Patton's solution was to convert about five percent of non-combat personnel into infantry replacements.

While XX Corps was still dealing with the reduction of Metz, Eddy's XII Corps continued its advance on the Saar River. The 4th Armored Division was teamed with the 26th Division on the right flank and, during the course

A squad from the 50th Armored Infantry Battalion, 6th Armored Division, takes a breather in a captured German trench during the fighting near Puttelange on November 26, 1944. The reinforced trench is typical of the type of fieldworks built by Wehrkreis XII in Lorraine as part of the West-Stellung program in the autumn of 1944. (NARA)

An M4A3(76mm) of the 6th Armored Division disabled by a German mine between Hellimer and Grostenquin on November 25, 1944. It has become thoroughly trapped in the mud. (NARA)

of the last two weeks of November, pushed out from the Dieuze area towards Saare-Union. This attack was affected ultimately by developments in the neighboring XV Corps sector of Seventh US Army. The American attacks into the Saverne Gap were pushing along the boundary of AOK 1 and AOK 19 and were so threatening that Balck was able to secure the Panzer-Lehr-Division from the OKW strategic reserve. Berlin finally had agreed to the request on November 23 with a mission to drive deep into XV Corps' flank in an attempt to redeem the deepening crisis in Alsace with "decisive results." At the time, the Panzer-Lehr-Division was rebuilding for the Ardennes offensive, and had a tank strength of 34 PzKpfw IVs and 38 Panthers. The lead elements of the Panzer-Lehr-Division struck parts of the 114th Infantry, 44th Division. However, CCB 4th Armored Division had already been operating near the junction of XII and XV Corps and was able to intervene.

As in the case of Patton's tank units, Panzer-Lehr-Division had considerable difficulty operating its tanks in the mud, and its offensive punch depended on fresh and inexperienced Panzergrenadiers. The fighting between the 53rd Armored Infantry Battalion and 1./Panzergrenadier-Regiment 902 in the village of Baerendorf went badly for the Germans. A determined defense by US troops in the sector dealt the Panzer-Lehr-Division such a setback that OB West commander, Generalfeldmarschall Gerd Rundstedt, ordered the Panzer-Lehr-Division to go over to the defensive, reinforced with elements of the 25. Panzergrenadier-Division. In difficult and soggy ground conditions, the armored infantry of the 4th Armored Division ground their way through the German defenses, finally reaching the outskirts of Saare-Union by the end of November. In a series of seesaw battles, Sarre-Union changed hands several times in the first few days of December, finally being captured on December 4 by the 37th Tank Battalion, 4th Armored Division, and the 104th Infantry. The fighting in this sector eventually petered out as OB West needed to withdraw the Panzer units for participation in the planned Ardennes offensive only a few weeks away. The 4th Armored Division was so battered from its continual autumn campaigns that it was finally pulled out of the line on December 7 for refitting.

The Seventh US Army November offensive cut off AOK 1 and AOK 19, forcing Berlin to dip into its Ardennes reserve in an attempt to restore the situation. On November 23, 1944, the Panzer-Lehr-Division began a counterattack from Sarre-Union but was beaten back when the 4th Armored Division launched a flank attack with its Combat Command B from Fénétrange. This Panther Ausf. G was knocked out during the fighting near Schalbach on November 25 with the 114th Infantry, a bazooka hit evident on the hull side immediately below the turret. (NARA)

The task facing the left wing of XII Corps was significantly different as this sector was dominated by swathes of the Maginot Line fortifications. The 6th Armored Division was used in concentrated fashion to push up the road from Morhange towards Remmering-les-Puttelange in the Maginot Line belt. The attack against dug-in elements of the 17. SS-Panzergrenadier-Division and the left flank of the 11. Panzer-Division was very slow moving owing to the soggy ground conditions as well as an extensive and effective West-Stellung field fortification belt. Balck wanted to withdraw the battered 11. Panzer-Division to the rear to refit it and re-assign it as the army reserve, so fresh troops were brought in from the 15. Panzergrenadier-Division to hold this sector. A combined attack by the 6th Armored Division and elements of the 35th Division finally secured Saint-Jean-Rohrbach on November 22. The month ended with the 6th Armored Division and 35th Division along the Maderbach River, about 27 miles (43km) from the start line three weeks earlier at the start of the offensive. The actions cost the 6th Armored Division 94 tanks of which about 30 were complete losses, but most of the casualties were due to tanks becoming bogged down in the sea of mud brought on by the autumn rain and snow. German losses in the sector were severe as well, with 73 tanks and assault guns being lost to the 6th Armored Division on this front in three weeks of fighting, a heavy toll given the impoverished state of the German Panzer units.

On December 4, the attack resumed in this sector by the 35th and 80th Infantry Divisions and the 6th Armored Division with the aim of securing Sarreguemines on the Saar River. In two days of fighting, the 35th Division and 6th Armored Division advanced to the western bank of the Saar and had a toehold in Sarreguemines. The push over the Saar was conducted to the northeast of Sarreguemines by the 35th and 26th Divisions aiming towards Zweibrucken. The 26th Division had a particularly tough assignment as its sector was infested with Maginot Line fortifications. The advance reached the outer perimeter of the Westwall by December 17 when news from the Ardennes brought further operations to a halt.

XX CORPS ADVANCES BEYOND METZ

Walker had kept the 10th Armored Division free of commitments to the reduction of Metz in the expectation that this would be his primary exploitation force towards the Saar River. Once free of the Moselle bridgeheads by the third week of November, the division began an advance with two combat commands towards the Westwall. The sector that the 10th Armored Division was approaching was the Orschloz-Riegel-Stellung (Orschloz Switch Position), one of the densest sectors of the Westwall, which had been further amplified by the West-Stellung program in the autumn of 1944. It was intended to block the so-called "Saar–Moselle Triangle," an entry point into Germany at the border of France and Luxembourg that was bounded by the Moselle River on one side and the Saar on the other, with the apex at Trier. Besides this east–west defense line, there was also a new Saar-Höhen-Stellung (Saar Heights Line) created as part of the new West-Stellung in the autumn of 1944 immediately across the German frontier to the west of the Saar River, and in front of the main belt of the Westwall.

Walker had originally hoped to use the 83rd Division in this action as well, but Bradley had attached so many strings to the use of this division that, in the end, it remained out of action. As a result, CCA, 10th Armored Division, began to grind into the Orschloz-Riegel-Stellung on November 19, while CCB began its attacks against the Saar-Höhen-Stellung. It soon became evident that more infantry was necessary, and the 358th Infantry, 90th Division, began to reinforce the CCA attack though with scant effect. The 10th Armored Division became stalled once it reached the fortified German defensive lines and lacked the dedicated engineer equipment to penetrate extensive fields of dragon's teeth and other obstructions.

Riflemen of the 10th Armored Infantry Battalion, 4th Armored Division, move across a muddy field in Lorraine on December 2, 1944. (NARA)

The two neighboring infantry divisions made steady but slow progress following the capture of Metz. Both the 90th and 95th Division, pushed on towards the Saar-Höhen-Stellung through the final week of November, encountering numerous rearguards but few major defense actions. The Germans staged occasional counterattacks from behind the defense lines such as an attack by a *Kampfgruppe* of the 21. Panzer-Division against the 1/377th Infantry in Saint-Barbara on November 29. The pressure from these two divisions all along the line forced Knobelsdorff at midnight on November 30 to order the right wing of AOK 1 based around the 19. Volksgrenadier-Division to abandon the Saar-Höhen-Stellung and pull back over the Saar River to the Westwall. Knobelsdorff was severely criticized by Rundstedt for this order, but he had been instructed by Balck to avoid the destruction of the 19. Volksgrenadier-Division on the western side of the Saar, and he had no alternatives to accomplishing this except by withdrawal in view of the complete lack of additional resources to reinforce the Saar-Höhen-Stellung. By the first days of December, the 95th Division was on the doorsteps of Saarlautern.

The most dramatic episode in the advance occurred in early December 1944, when an American artillery observation plane discovered an intact bridge over the Saar connecting the main part of Saarlautern to the northern suburbs. In the pre-dawn hours of December 3, the 1/379th Infantry crossed the river in assault boats from outside the city and the crossing went unobserved because of a noisy artillery preparation in nearby sectors. Company B, accompanied by engineers, raced to the bridge and found a German light tank guarding the bridge but the occupants asleep. Awakened by the clambering of American infantrymen on the tank, the crew tried to radio an alarm and to detonate the bridge charges, but were quickly killed as were the guards at the opposite side of the bridge. The remainder of the 379th Infantry occupied the town. The intact bridge allowed the dispatch of a platoon from the 607th Tank Destroyer Battalion for reinforcement. After artillery strikes failed to down the bridge, the Germans attempted to demolish it by racing a few tanks towards the bridge, loaded with explosives. The lead tank was destroyed, putting an end to this curious attempt. In the afternoon, Kampfgruppe Spreu was formed, based on Panzergrenadier-Regiment 192 of

A platoon from the 35th Division passes by a wrecked German truck on the outskirts of Puttelange on December 5, 1944, a day after the town was taken from the 17. SS-Panzergrenadier-Division. (NARA)

An M10 3in. GMC of the 654th Tank Destroyer Battalion is seen peering around the corner of a house in Habkirchen while supporting the 134th Infantry, 35th Division, during the fighting with the 36. Volksgrenadier-Division along the Saar River on December 15, 1945. (NARA)

the 21. Panzer-Division and dispatched to swing around the flanks of the 379th Infantry to cut off the bridgehead. This counterattack failed as well.

Rundstedt was furious when he learned of the American foothold over the Saar, and ordered AOK 1 to destroy the bridge and push the Americans off the east bank of the Saar at all costs. A whitewashing of the incident by Heeresgruppe G concluded that the Americans had secured the bridge by a ruse using a captured German tank, and the matter was dropped. However, AOK 1 was obliged to follow Rundstedt's orders and another attack on the bridge was staged by Kampfgruppe Lier, based around a battalion from the 21. Panzer-Division including a few tanks, reinforced by a company of engineers and 300 trainees from the AOK 1 Waffenschule (weapons school). They attacked around 1000hrs on December 4, but the tanks were shot up by the 90mm GMCs of the 607th Tank Destroyer Battalion and the untrained infantry was dispersed with small-arms fire.

For the Germans, the situation in the XX Corps sector only grew worse when the 90th Division seized another bridgehead over the Saar near Patchen, a few miles to the northwest of Saarlautern and within the Westwall defensive belt. The 90th fought its way into the neighboring town of Dillingen, also ensconced in the Westwall defensive belt. Hitler was enraged by the news, and ordered punitive measures for any soldiers involved in the loss of Westwall defense works. Knobelsdorff was relieved from AOK 1 command because of the Saarlautern bridge incident, though Rundstedt softened the

Saarlautern was located within the Westwall defense zone, and so there were many pillboxes located inside the town. These two buildings at the Saalautern railroad station are in fact cleverly camouflaged bunkers. (NARA)

blow by allowing him to transfer to a fortress command in Germany and ascribing the demotion to his worsening medical condition after harsh service in Russia. The Heeresgruppe G chief of staff Oberst Friedrich von Mellenthin was the next to go, and Balck lasted only until December 23. Hitler finally authorized reinforcements for the Saarlautern sector.

Armeeoberkommando 1 continued the series of counterattacks against the bridgeheads, including an assault on Pachten by a section of four PzKpfw IV tanks and two engineer companies from the 11. Panzer-Division on December 7 and a large attack by the newly arrived 719. Infanterie-Division on December 8. Even though the German counterattacks were unsuccessful and costly, a vicious stalemate soon developed all along the XX Corps front. The US divisions by this stage were short of infantry with the 95th Division requesting 2,000 replacements; combat efficiency was rated as 61 percent. By the second week of December, the 90th Division's combat efficiency was rated as only 43 percent owing to the heavy infantry casualties. This area was one of the strongest sectors of the Westwall, and the towns east of the Saar had extensive and well-designed fortified positions. The 90th Division gradually ground through the defensive works in Dillingen, hoping to link up this bridgehead with the Saarlautern bridgehead to the southeast. It all proved for naught as on December 19, Patton ordered the division to withdraw across the Saar. A German counteroffensive had erupted days before in a quiet sector of the Ardennes, and Third US Army was taking the first steps to relieve a little-known town called Bastogne.

THE CAMPAIGN IN RETROSPECT

Patton's campaign in Lorraine in the autumn of 1944 is often described as his least successful venture. In contrast to the brilliant advances of August and early September, the November–December fighting was a series of exasperating and brutish skirmishes which finally overcame the Metz fortified zone, but barely reached the Westwall by the time the Ardennes offensive intervened. Patton's frustrations in Lorraine were evident in his jeremiad: "I hope that in the final settlement of the war, the Germans retain Lorraine. I can imagine no greater burden than to be the owner of this nasty country where it rains every day and where the whole wealth of the people consists in assorted manure piles."

Third US Army claimed to have inflicted 152,000 casualties on Heeresgruppe G in the October–December battles, at a cost of 36,800 of its own casualties. While the claims may be high, the German losses were substantial; Third US Army collected nearly 25,600 prisoners of war in November alone. The territorial gains were not particularly impressive compared with the summer battles, with the Third US Army advancing to a depth of about 30 miles (50km) in the November–December attacks.

German commanders were less critical of the fighting by Walker's XX Corps at Metz than of the failure of Eddy's XII Corps to make more dramatic progress. Some argued that Patton should have assembled his armor in a tank-heavy corps and then punched through the weak German lines in a bold dash for the Rhine. Both Balck and Knobelsdorff expected XII Corps to constitute Patton's focal point in Operation *Madison*, and were surprised when instead it was the infantry of Walker's XX Corps that received the primary role in the attack.

Patton's performance in Lorraine should be assessed by the resources available and the weather and terrain factors. It is also helpful to judge them against the progress of other Allied field armies at the same time. The Third US Army in November–December 1944 did not have the priority or resources afforded it in August 1944. It had shrunken from four corps to only two corps. Air support was a shadow of what it had been in the summer with only 3,500 sorties in November compared with 12,300 in August. This was in part due to the poor weather, but also the diversion of resources to the main effort in the Aachen–Stolberg corridor. Weather and terrain certainly had a far more serious impact on the progress of Patton's Third US Army than did resources. The exceptionally wet November weather greatly complicated operations along the Moselle owing to extensive flooding. The more serious impact was in the XII Corps sector where the sodden soil created "a front one tank wide."

Under these soggy conditions, Patton's experienced 4th and 6th Armored Divisions were hamstrung by their inability to exploit their mobility. Operations had to be conducted along major roads owing to the impassability of the muddy terrain for much of the November–December fighting. Confinement to roads meant that the German AOK 1 was able to mass its limited resources, including mines and anti-tank weapons, along key avenues. Small villages could serve as bastions that had to be methodically reduced since they could not be avoided. This tactical problem was not confined to Patton's Third Army and also was evident in the armored attacks of Bradley's First and Ninth US Armies during the Operation *Queen* offensive in the Aachen–Stolberg corridor in November. Nor was it peculiar to US tank units. Much of the misfortune suffered by the German 1. SS-Panzerarmee in its initial attack in the Ardennes at the start of the Battle of the Bulge was due to the same tactical dilemma. The German attacks were forced to use the roads because of the sodden ground conditions, obliging the Panzer spearheads to fight savage little sieges for towns at key road junctions such as Krinkelt-Rocherath, Stoumont and La Gleize. The spectacular Panzer advances in the Ardennes did not occur until after December 22 when the ground finally froze, enabling tank units to move off the road and avoid the time-consuming, nasty little battles for every little village along the major roads.

Even if the armored divisions of Eddy's XII Corps had reached the Westwall sooner under more favorable weather conditions, it is by no means clear that penetration through these defenses would have been assured. The First US Army penetrated the Westwall quickly in September 1944 on the outskirts of Aachen largely because they were derelict and unmanned. This was not the case in the autumn of 1944 because the German army quickly revived the Westwall under the West-Stellung program and enhanced the anti-tank defenses. Third US Army tank units were not well equipped to deal with these tank barriers as was evident when the 10th Armored Division faced the Orscholz-Riegel-Stellung in December 1944 in the XX Corps sector. Penetration of these anti-tank belts required tools and tactics that took time and experience to accumulate and this was the Third US Army's first taste of these defenses.

Some of the criticism of Patton's campaign in Lorraine has been rooted in the overoptimism that flavored US Army decision-making in the early autumn of 1944. After the rout of the German Army in August 1944 and early September, there was a widespread perception that the Wehrmacht was finished and that the exceptional pace of the late summer offensives would continue. This attitude was most evident in the hasty decision to storm Fort Driant with such inadequate forces. Third US Army plans continued to contain a strain of this exuberance, still talking about a Rhine crossing at Mainz in its Operation *Madison* plans. This overconfidence quickly ran into the reality of the revitalized Germany Army in the early autumn of 1944, often dubbed the "Wunder am der Westwall" (the Westwall miracle). It can certainly be argued that the German defensive prowess in Lorraine in the autumn of 1944 was more the norm for the Wehrmacht in World War II than the disastrous "Void" of August–September 1944.

Indeed, the overwhelming impression left by the Lorraine campaign was the remarkable ability of the German Army to do so much with so little. Armeeoberkommando 1 had few first-rate units at its disposal, and those that it did have, such as the 11. Panzer-Division, had been beaten and battered by months of fighting. Much of this success can be attributed to both the Lorraine fortifications and the success of Wehrkreis XII in providing a steady stream of replacements and supplies to the field armies. Both American and German commanders were wrong to dismiss the potential of the Metz fortified belt in September 1944. While the forts certainly could not have been the centerpiece of defense planning, they proved to be an effective backbone for German defense efforts, especially in view of the poor quality of many of the units in this sector. Another misunderstood aspect of the German defense effort was the extensive West-Stellung field fortification effort in August–November 1944 which created several defensive lines behind Metz and which slowed the US advance in November–December 1944 with extensive tank obstacles and minefields. This was not part of the Westwall as was often assumed but a large, deliberate and new program. The West-Stellung program was a vital crutch for an increasingly bedraggled Wehrmacht.

The performance of Patton's Third US Army in Lorraine should also be judged in comparison with other Allied field armies in the same time frame. In Montgomery's 21st Army Group in the Netherlands, the Canadian First Army fought a brutal struggle against AOK 15 to clear the Scheldt. It faced many of the same constraints as Patton regarding difficult terrain, poor weather and extensive German field fortifications that greatly slowed their progress. The neighboring British Second Army made little effort in the Reichswald at this time, supporting the Scheldt operation instead. On the German frontier north of the Ardennes, Bradley's 12th Army Group, including Ninth US Army and First US Army, staged Operation *Queen* in November 1944 at roughly the same time as Operation *Madison*. These two field armies had priority over Patton for supplies and air support yet they had conspicuously little success even though Bradley had hoped that the operation would be as decisive as Operation *Cobra*, the Normandy breakout. The only Allied field armies that had more impressive success than Patton in the autumn of 1944 was Devers' 6th Army Group in Alsace. The stunning success of Patch's Seventh US Army in overcoming the formidable Vosges Mountains and the costly victory of de Tassigny's First French Army in the Belfort Gap are frequently overlooked. Their success was in part due to Balck's conviction that Patton's Third US Army posed more of a threat to Heeresgruppe G than Devers' army group. As a result, Balck favored AOK 1 in Lorraine instead of AOK 19 in Alsace in the allotment of units and resources.

Patton's reputation in Lorraine has been tarnished more by the small but dramatic setback at Fort Driant in October 1944 than enhanced by the clear success of Operation *Madison* in November. What is often forgotten was that Heeresgruppe G was so decisively defeated in November–December 1944, that Patton was able to pull two of his corps out of Lorraine in late December 1944 and send them to Bastogne with so little risk of counteraction by AOK 1. Indeed, when the Wehrmacht planned the Heeresgruppe G Operation *Nordwind* in January 1945, AOK 1 was deliberately omitted from the scheme owing to its shattered condition. This would become all too evident in March 1945 when Patton's Third US Army returned to the Saar and decisively crushed AOK 1 in the catastrophic "Rhine Rat Race" through the Saar–Palatinate to the Rhine.

THE BATTLEFIELD TODAY

Most of the Metz forts returned to French Army control after the war and, with a few exceptions, were generally restricted to the public. Some were used by joint headquarters, such as the Caserne Grandmaison in the Queuleu suburb of Metz as seen here. This gives a good impression of the typical German caserne designs in the Metz forts as well as the usual dry moat and counterscarp walls. (NARA)

Metz and the surrounding area of Lorraine are filled with military architecture, but there are few museums devoted to the 1944 fighting. The many fortresses in the Metz area are the most enduring reminder of the autumn 1944 battles. However, access to the most interesting of these such as Fort Driant and Fort Koenigsmacker have been restricted since the end of World War II as property of the French Army. In the 1950s, Fort Jeanne d'Arc was converted into the Moselle Common Area Control (MCAC) and was eventually abandoned in the late 1990s. These days, Fort Driant is abandoned and overgrown; Fort Koenigsmacker is so derelict and dangerous that it remains off limits. In recent years, some of the other old bases that have been abandoned have been turned over to museums. There are excellent displays at Feste Wagner (Groupe fortifié l'Aisne/Fort Verny) south of Metz which is operated by the Association pour la Découverte de la Fortification Messine

(ADFM). Although it did not take part in the battle for Metz, the Groupe Fortifié Guentrange (Feste Obergentringen) is well preserved and gives an excellent impression of the configuration of the Mosel-Stellung forts. Several other Metz forts are accessible to the public though not restored, including Fort Illange, Fort Gambetta and Fort Queuleu (Feste Goeben). There are also numerous Maginot Line forts in Lorraine.

Metz remains filled with reminders of its recent troubled history. Temple Neuf was built on the site of an old bastion on the Île de Petit Saulcy in the Moselle River by Kaiser Wilhelm II starting in 1901 as a Protestant church for the expanding German fortress garrison in the city. (Author)

FURTHER READING

Documentation of the US Army in the Lorraine campaign is ample, starting with Cole's excellent campaign history in the US Army Green Book series. In addition, there is a wide range of published corps and divisional histories. Books on the German defense of Lorraine are scant, though there is an extensive collection of reports written by German officers immediately after the war for the US Army's "Foreign Military Studies" program as listed here. Archival records for the German army in 1944 are spotty though the US National Archives and Records Administration (NARA) does have the Heeresgruppe G war diary which contains a great deal of useful material. Tactical detail of the Metz fighting is largely lacking owing to the destruction of the Festung Metz records in November 1944. Nevertheless, some details remain; for example a short history of the Fahnenjunkerschule VI Metz, which was found by US counterintelligence officers in the Gestapo files in Metz and now located in the XX Corps G-2 (intelligence) records at NARA. The G-2 records of the US Army's 5th, 90th and 95th Divisions also have a wealth of detail about German units in the Metz fighting and some of the only extant accounts of the Fort Driant actions from the German perspective.

US Army Reports

After Action Report, Third US Army, 1 August 1944–9 May 1945 (1945)

The Reduction of Fortress Metz: XX Corps Operational Report 1 September–6 December 1944 (1945)

Report on Operations Conducted by the 95th Infantry Division in the Vicinity of Metz, France and Saarlautern, Germany during the period 8 November–3 December 1944 (1945)

The Effectiveness of Third Phase Tactical Air Operation in the European Theater: 5 May 1944–8 May 1945 (Army Air Force Evaluation Board in the ETO: August 1945)

Fort Blaise, Verdun Group, Metz, France (No. 14, US Strategic Bombing Survey, Physical Damage Division: January 1947)

Barnes, Harry, *The Operations of the 1st Battalion, 358th Infantry (90th Infantry Division) at Fort Koenigsmacker, North of Thionville, France 9–11 November 1944* (Infantry School, 1948)

Barnes, John, *Operations of G Company, 379th Infantry (95th Infantry Division) in Breaching the Maginot Line in the Vicinity of Fort Jean d'Arc, 14–15 November 1944* (Infantry School, 1950)

Bussolati, Emile, *The Operations of the 1st Battalion, 2nd Infantry (5th Infantry Division) in the Crossing of the Seille River and Subsequent Attack on the Town of Louvigny, south of Metz, France, 9 November 1944* (Infantry School: 1950)

Cantey, J., et. al., *The 10th US Armored Division in the Saar–Moselle Triangle* (Armor School: 1949)

Edwards, Meyer, et al., *Armor in the attack of fortified positions* (Armor School: 1950)

Glick, John, *Operations of the 736th Field Artillery Battalion, XX Corps Artillery in the Capture of the City of Metz, France, 2–20 November 1944* (Infantry School: 1949)

Goers, William, *The Operations of Company E, 358th Infantry (90th Division) at Cattenom (Moselle River Crossing) 9–12 November 1944* (Infantry School: 1949)

Kercher, Ferris, *The Operations of the 10th Infantry (5th Infantry Division) in the Vicinity of Arnaville, Southwest of Metz, France, 10–16 September, 1944* (Infantry School: 1948)

Ludwikosky, John, *735th Tank Battalion in the Reduction of Metz* (Armor School: 1950)

Mabry, Ned, *Reduction of the Fortified City of Metz, France by the XX Corps, 9–22 November 1944* (Infantry School, 1949)

Peterson, Evar, et al., *Armor vs. Mud and Mines: 4th Armored Division in the Saare–Moselle Area* (Armor School: 1950)

Stephenson, R., et al., *The Battle of Metz* (Combat Studies Institute Battle Book 13-A: 1984)

Sullivan, John, *The Operations of Company G, 2nd Infantry (5th Infantry Division) in the Reduction of Fortress Metz, 6–15 September 1944, Amanvillers–Verneville Action* (Infantry School: 1947)

Foreign Military Studies

Britzelmayr, Karl, *History of the 19. VGD: 15 Sep 44–27 Apr 45* (B-527)

Eckstein, Otto, *LXXXIX Corps: 20 Sep–23 Nov 44*, (B-760, B-790)

Einem, Kurt von, *Engagements of the XIII-SS-Corps in Lorraine: 1 Sep 44–15 Nov 44* (B-412)

Emmerich, Albert, *First Army: 15 Sep–20 Dec 1944* (B-363, B-443)

Höhne, Gustav, *LXXXIX Army Corps Combat History: Saarbrucken and Weissenburg Maps* (B-075)

Hold, Kurt, *Organization and Composition of the First Army: 11 Aug 44 to 14 Feb 45* (B-732, B-821)

Kittel, Heinrich, *462. Volksgrenadier Division: 12 Nov–13 Dec 1944* (B-079)

Kohl, Otto, *First Army Rear Area: 1 Oct 44–21 May 45* (B-091)

Krause, Walter, *Defense of Metz 1–8 Sep 1944* (B-042)

Mantey, Willy, *First Army: 1 Sep–4 Dec 1944* (B-214, B-751)

Mühlen, Kurt, *559 VGD, The Rhineland Campaign: 15 Sep–21 Sep 44* (A-972)

Peschke, Kurt, *Defensive Combat of the LXXXIX Inf Corps in the lower Alsace and in the Westwall from 6 to 31 Dec 1944* (C-003)

Seemüller, Hugo, *Bericht über die Kämpfe des XIII.SS-AK in Lothringen in der Zeit vom 8.Nov.44 bis 12.Jan.45* (B-780)

——, *Battles of the 416 Infantry Division between the Moselle and the Saar from 5 Oct 1944 to 17 Feb 1945* (B-573)

Simon, Max, *Report on the Rhineland and Southern Germany Campaign* (B-487)

——, *XIII SS Inf Corps in the Lorraine Campaign* (ETHINT 33)

Tippelskirch, Kurt von, *First Army: 1–11 Nov 1944* (B-491, B-492)

Wietersheim, Wend von, *Employment of the 11. Panzerdivision in Lorraine* (B-364, B-416)

Books

The Fifth Infantry Division in the ETO (Battery Press: 1997)

The XX Corps: Its History and Service In World War II (XX Corps Association: 1947)

A History of the 90th Division in World War II (Battery Press: 1999)

Bettinger, Dieter, *Die Geschichte der HGru G Mai 1944 bis Mai 1945* (Helios: 2010)

Burtscher, Philippe, and Hoff, François, *Les fortifications allemandes d'Alsace-Lorraine 1870–1918*, (Histoire & Collections: 2008)

Caboz, René, *La Bataille de Nancy: Luneville-Chateau Salins-Faulquemont 25 aout au 17 novembre 1944* (Pierron: 1994)

Colby, John, *War from the Ground Up: The 90th Division in WWII* (Nortex: 1991)

Cole, Hugh, *The Lorraine Campaign* (US Army Historical Division: 1950)

Christoffel, Edgar, *Krieg am Westwall 1944/45* (Interbook: 1989)

Dyer, George, *XII Corps: Spearhead of Patton's Third Army* (XII Corps History Association: 1947)

Fontbonne, Rémi, *Les fortifications allemandes de Metz et de Thionville 1871–1918* (Serpenoise: 2006)

Fuermann, George, and Cranz, Edward, *Ninety-Fifth Infantry Division History 1918–1946* (Battery Press: 1988)

Gabel, Christopher, *The Lorraine Campaign: An Overview September–December 1944* (Combat Studies Institute: 1985)

Kemp, Anthony, *Metz 1944* (Heimdal: 2003)

——, *The Unknown Battle: Metz 1944* (Stein & Day: 1981)

Mangin, Pierre, *L'armée Patton à l'assaut des forts de Metz* (Typo Lorraine: 2000)

Rickard, John, *Patton at Bay: The Lorraine Campaign, September to December 1944* (Praeger: 1999)

Rolf, Rudi, *Die Deutsche Panzerfortifikation: Die Panzerfesten von Metz und ihre Vorgeschichte* (Biblio: 1991)

Spires, David, *Air Power for Patton's Army: The XIX Tactical Air Command in the Second World War* (USAF History: 2002)

INDEX

References to illustrations are shown in **bold**.